"The Teacher"

The Public Years of the Baron Eugene Fersen - Volume 1

"The Teacher"

The Public Years of the Baron Eugene Fersen - Volume 1

THE LIGHTBEARERS PUBLISHING, Inc.

a division of

THE SCIENCE OF BEING WORLD CENTER

No part of this book may be reproduced in any manner

whatsoever without the written permission of

THE LIGHTBEARERS PUBLISHING, Inc.

or

THE LIGHTBEARERS SCIENCE OF BEING WORLD CENTER

and its Next Generation AHLB'S.

www.scienceofbeing.com

Copyright © 2012 By THE LIGHTBEARERS PUBLISHING, Inc.

All rights to the information in this book

are reserved and protected by copyright Law.

ISBN-13: 978-0985318604
ISBN-10: 0985318600

To those noble Men and Women, whose elightened
Courage and untiring Efforts made possible
Progress on Earth, do I dedicate this book.

Eugene Kersen

DEDICATION:

**TO PASS THE LIGHT OF THIS WISDOM
TO THE HUMANITY OF THE SIXTH RACE -
"THE TEACHER."**

> This Light is given to You
> In All Love and Joy
> Bear It to the world in the
> Same Spirit as You Receive It
> And Its Glowing Flame shall Wax
> In Radiance to the Empyrean
> Of Eternal Light.

Appreciation and Great Gratitude's:

The Science Of Being ~ Lightbearers World Center would like to express its deepest appreciation and gratitude to those who have supported and worked tirelessly to bring Volume I "The Teacher," the public years of The Baron Eugene Fersen's unpublished and rare archival knowledge to Humanity for this the New Age.

The Lightbearers 'Next Generation,' World Center would like to acknowledge with Great Gratitude Laura Taylor-Jensen Chief Correspondence and the public representative Acting Head Lightbearer of the World Center for whereby her skill to hear Destiny's call, the Lightbearers World Center's spark would not have been ignited for the Next Generation Lightbearers; we are forever grateful for your tenacity, selflessness, generosity of compassion towards the people of our World and your unwavering Loyalty to the Teachings. And to Eugene Loher Acting Head Lightbearer – Science Of Being LB World Center who upholds the memories of those who came before us, Sharon Tiffany - Columbia Gorge Interpretive Center Museum – for their continued support in the care of the Baron Eugene Fersen's antiquities, Diane King for her family's loving donation, Barry and Margaret Sue Wright CLB's of the Lightbearers Center VA - for their Publishing contributions, dedication to the Teachings and their friendship, Valerie L. Dillon – editing and key stroking, Theresa Jump for her expert key stroking and content organization, Phyllis Uitti-Maslin – Photography, Steve Smith at Classic Insights – Cover design. To all the Elder Lightbearers that came before us and most importantly the Baron Eugene Fersen for coming to the World to share with us his Life, Intelligence, the Truth and Love on "All" Planes and to the Great Law and Principle for creating and giving us Life with the guidance of our Higher Mind so we may have the Flame of Inspiration to guide us back to the Sacred Grove.

"May The Flame Of Love and Inspiration Always Light Your Way,"

The Science Of Being ~ Lightbearers World Center

BARON EUGENE FERSEN

Baron Eugene Fersen was the eldest son of the Grand Duchess of Russia, known as Marie Olga Alexandrovna of Russia. His mother knew before his birth that he was to be a guiding light for the people of this World; she called him "Svetozar," meaning "The Lightbearer," which Eugene began penning publicly when he volunteered in the Russian Red Cross during the war. Eugene's mother saw to it that her son had the proper teachers and education that would assist and support the Absolute Eternal Aspects of his Soul so as to fulfill his divine destiny.

We can only speak briefly about Eugene's father as those were the instructions and wishes left for us by the Elder Lightbearers. What we can share is what Eugene himself publicly spoke of when speaking of his father's side of the family, that, "he was a direct descendent of Count Axel Fersen." Eugene's grandfather, on his mother's side, was King Alexander the II of Russia. Eugene's uncle, by marriage, was Count Leo Tolstoy, the writer famously known for his renowned literary works "War and Peace," and "Anna Karenina." Tolstoy was one of Gandhi's greatest influences and friend. Eugene's half-sister was Queen Marie of Romania, the daughter-in-law of Queen Victoria of England. Eugene had a very close relationship with his half-sister Queen Marie; they spent many of their adult years together in the US and her daughter, Princess Marie, stayed with Eugene until his death.

In 1901, Eugene came to the United States with his Mother the Grand Duchess and in 1904 began sharing his message and teachings known as "The Science Of Being." In 1906 through 1921 the Baron Eugene was investigated by the U.S. Government's Justice Department as a "Possible Radical." Eugene was a Russian Royal teaching what the U.S. Government termed as "radical religious thinking;" this investigation accelerated during World War I, 1914-1918. In late September of 1921, the United States Government closed their investigation on Eugene. By early 1923, the U.S. Government allowed Eugene to become an American

Citizen and granted him free reign to publish, through the American Press, his already acclaimed lessons, "The Science Of Being".

Before Eugene was sworn in as an American, the proceeding judge cautioned the Baron Eugene, that once he took the oath to become an American Citizen, he would no longer be able to take the Royal Throne he was born to empire. Eugene knew his purpose and mission wasn't to reign over Humankind but to assume a modest seat of service for the spiritual progress of 'All,' Humanity."

The Baron Eugene Fersen was intimately associated with the world's most eminent teachers, scientists and philosophers; some of his most profound personal teachers were from the lineage of the Great Magi. In the late 1800s through the mid 1900s Eugene taught or influenced many of the great teachers who are now responsible for the greatest-human-healing-potential movement of our time: Charles Haanel (The Master Key System,) Dr. Hotema, Elizabeth Towne (Publisher of Nautilus Magazine,) Wallace D. Wattles (The Science Of Getting Rich and The Science Of Being Well,) Edgar Cayce, Annie Besant (Translator of the Bhagavad Gita, Theosophist, and Leader of Woman's Rights,) Huna Max Freedom Long (great teacher of the Huna ways and teacher to the founders of the Course In Miracles,) Charles Fillmore (Founder of The Unity Church,) Samuel Clemens (author of Mark Twain), William Walker Atkinson (one of the three Initiates of the Kybalion,) Nikola Tesla, Manly P. Hall, Jon Peniel, and the list goes on. Rudolph Steiner himself was touched by Eugene's teachings and had him as a guest speaker/teacher in the Steiner Schools whenever Eugene could be available.

The Baron Eugene Fersen taught anyone who had a genuine interest in the "Science Of Being," the Truth, and the path to spiritual and human liberation. At the time of his parting into the Great Beyond in 1956, the Baron Eugene Fersen had personally instructed well over 20,000 students and at that time more than 100,000 people worldwide had read or been exposed to the teachings of the "Science Of Being." These teachings today are regarded as some of the most inspiring literary works in the study and education of Quantum Science, Spiritual Science, Human Enlightenment and the study of the Soul.

The Baron Eugene, came to share with us the Truth of these wisdoms with the hope that Humankind would free themselves from the myths that held them hostage and bound them to an un-liberated existence here on

Earth. He shared that there are still vast amounts of profound wisdoms that remain veiled from Humankind because the un-liberated subconsciousness mind had become resistant to comprehending those truths. He knew and had faith that as humans enlightened their bodies, minds and raised their Spiritual Vibrations as they lived in the physical world, more would be revealed to them.

Baron Eugene Fersen, "The Teacher of the Teachers," gave to the world with an open heart, mind and spirit these profound truths, his life's purpose, and his "seat-of-power and privilege." He believed deeply that all of Humankind regardless of class, creed, gender or difference should have access to these great wisdoms that were once only privy to the rich and powerful. He acquired, as he lived, the manna all alchemists were truly looking for, the peak of spiritual attainment, whereas one's body, mind and spirit reaches Its highest vibrational aspects of spiritual evolution in physical form; whereas Spirit matter becomes one with Its pure Soul.

The Baron Eugene Fersen's life purpose was to bring to Humankind the lost principles of our first Primal Ancestors so as to assist Humanity to complete their tasks to awaken,' to the 'All,' knowing latent scintillating star that resides within each of their Absolute Eternal Souls.

The Teacher, Volume I

Table Of Contents

SECTION I:
LETTERS FROM SCIENCE OF BEING STUDENTS 1920-1942

Portrait of "The Teacher," Named Baron Eugene Fersen / 2

Letters From Students 1920-1942 / 3

SECTION II:
SCIENCE OF BEING VIBRATIONS, MEDITATIONS & EXCERCISES

Meditation "Manifesting All Qualities and Powers" / 12

"Vibrations" / 13

"Vibrations" / 14

The Mental Contact with Universal Life Energy and the Star Exercise / 15

Rejuvenation Exercise / 18

The Sphere / 20

Our Father / 22

SECTION III:
ORIGINAL PUBLIC LECTURE ANNOUNCEMENTS &
THE PUBLIC LECTURES BY THE BARON EUGENE FERSEN

*The New Era or the Coming Order Dawning Now Upon Mankind
How To Prepare Oneself for the Changing Standard of Life and The World Crisis* / 24

The Explanation of the Science of Being Teachings? / 26

What is GOD? / 28

What is Science? / 29

Democracy and the Land of Freedom / 30

Life as I See It / 33

1933 Winter Course in the Science of Being - First Lesson / 34

1933 Winter Course in the Science of Being - Second Lesson / 40

1933 Winter Course in the Science of Being - Third Lesson / 51

1933 Winter Course in the Science of Being - Fourth Lesson / 60

1933 Winter Course in the Science of Being - Fifth Lesson / 70

Spiritual Lesson – December 29, 1933 / 81

Do the Dead Come Back To Live Again? / 84

Third Friday Assembly / 88

Lesson given by the Baron Eugene Fersen / 92

Notes of the Baron Eugene Fersen's Lecture by L. Anciaux / 100

Six Lessons given by the Baron Eugene Fersen / 106

Jealousy, Hatred, Doubt / 114

A Day of Darkness and of Light / 116

Account of Lecture by Eugene Fersen / 126

The End / 131

Original Public Lecture Announcements of Eugene Fersen, L. / 133

SECTION IV:
SCIENCE OF BEING ~ LIGHTBEARERS ART & INFORMATION

Information for the Reader / 178

Lightbearer Emblems / 180

The Mighty Spirit / 184

The Awakening / 186

The Morning Star / 188

Section I:

Letters from Science Of Being Students 1920-1942

"There is nothing greater on earth than to be a teacher."

~ Eugene Fersen

Portrait of "The Teacher," Named Baron Eugene Fersen
Written by L. Anciaux

Seated on the platform between the NCLB and the organizing secretary for the Montreal Lightbearers was THE LIGHTBEARER, Eugene Fersen, a man of arresting personality, a trifle above the average height with a carriage, chest expansion and poise of manner which might well be the envy of others half his age. A man who has come to mean, to those who know and love him, a stimulus and an inspiration which mere words cannot express. For sheer courage and tenacity of purpose in the face of overwhelming obstacles he has no equal, and with all the love toward his fellows is mingled a penetrating shrewdness of judgement which forms a perfect balance.

His words have power to strike within us the lost chord of Truth and surely in his lecture tonight they produced an extraordinary effect, an effect which I am certain will still persist in others who in years to come shall read this and other accounts with understanding eyes, for it will take its place with the immortal literature of all time.

He began with his usual "Greetings Everybody," and gave what the early Christians called "Blessings," and which we now call "Vibrations." Slowly, very slowly this time he extended his arms and covered us in slow circles, like some master musician bringing to a grand rhythm the instruments under his baton, and indeed we could feel momently the surge of that POWER which we know as UNIVERSAL LIFE ENERGY as it flowed through us producing a state of harmony and peace which has to be experienced to be understood.

Letters From Students
1920-1942

Dear Mr. Fersen:

You will perhaps be interested to know what your course in "Science Of Being" has done for me.

Ever since I "stepped out on my own," I have been trying with a good deal of impatience and very little success to strike my own gait in the management of my affairs. I was always too cautious where I should have dared and too reckless where I should have been cautious, only I never knew it until afterward. Most of my moves were guesswork, because I didn't have the necessary foresight to make them anything else, and two-thirds of the time they were wrong.

Today just the reverse is true. Your course in "Science Of Being" gave me exactly the perspective I needed to wipe guesswork out of my experience. I may be able now to throw my energies completely in one direction or another with the absolute conviction that it is the right one. The true causes behind appearances are clear to me; I can go on with assurance because I can see my way, instead of simply fumbling along blindly and hoping I may be right.

The material value of your course to me even during this short time is clearly measured by the difference between where I was and where I am. The intangible values of personal satisfaction, confidence, freedom from worry, newly discovered and quickly unfolding abilities – all that may go to make a man pleased with what he finds inside him – have no yardstick dimensions. All I can say is that I appreciate them, in the true sense of that word, and am correspondingly grateful to you and to the "Science Of Being".

Sincerely yours,
Dr. S.T. Magnuson,
American Bank Bldg. Seattle Wn. (WA)

Dear Sir:

There is no price you could give me that would in any way take the place of what the lessons have done for me. I have not lost a day in the last year; my health is almost perfect. You may remember you treated me for a wry neck last year; my neck is straight now, and I am getting more joy out of life than I have ever done. I am mentally more alive than I have ever been-so you see, one could not ask for much more.

I am yours, sincerely,
Miss R. Finlaysun – Calgary, Alberta

Dear Mr. Fersen:

I have been told that I am a living monument to these teachings. From birth I had been very weak and nervous, and for years I was a semi-invalid. As medical science could give me no relief I took up the study of Metaphysics. For more than ten years I applied myself to the newer way of thinking, and while there was an improvement, it was not sufficient to keep me from feeling that life was a heavy burden. I was seldom free from pain, and weariness was my constant companion.

Thirteen months ago I heard of your teachings and took the course. After the physical chemicalization my health began to improve steadily. The application of these teachings has brought to me a vitality that I had not known before. Weakness is giving place to strength and from month to month I realize that I am steadily gaining. I am often told that I do not seem like the same person and I am surely a freer and happier one.

This sense of more abundant life is gratefully appreciated as is also the wider mental and spiritual outlook that the teachings have brought me. It is a wonderful teaching, demonstrable and practical, giving a reason for the hope that is in us and teaching us how man can truly "hitch his wagon to a star."

For your loving effort to bring this teaching to Humanity I am very grateful.

L.L. Davies.
Bremerton, Wn. (WA)

Dear Svetozar:

Permit me to express my sincere gratitude to you personally, as well as to The Lightbearers, for the wonderful service you have rendered me during your visit in Winnipeg.

If you, or anyone else, would have told me three weeks ago, what you could do for me, although I am a scientific agriculturist and as such come in very close contact with Nature, I would not only have doubted you, but would have pronounced it absolutely impossible. Today I am convinced beyond any doubt that your teachings are the only LOGICAL ones in the world and that, if followed with aims of high standard in mind, there is no glory too high to which any man or woman cannot aspire successfully.

I consider the year 1926 as the most successful year in my life, and I am able to go into the new year of 1927 enlightened with the Knowledge of Life, which is so essential to the spiritual and material success of any individual.

It is impossible to repay you in words or money for your services, but if there is anything that I can do in the future, all you have to do is call on me and I assure you that I will co-operate with you and your organization to the limit of my ability.

Wishing you Happy Holidays, and all kinds of success in your unselfish service to humanity.

I am Respectfully yours,
L. Herman
Winnipeg, Manitoba.

Dear Mr. Fersen:

I wish to tell you how deeply I appreciate the understanding gained through your teachings. By making the contact with Universal Energy as taught by "The Science Of Being" I have been able to help myself and others when difficulties have arisen. Just through one treatment the patient has been healed or much benefited.

Through the Star Exercise and Mental Contact my inner self is awakening and my latent powers are gradually developing, because where jealousy, fear and other negative conditions have been, a feeling of security, joy and love for all things is little by little becoming a part of my nature.

In my five years of mental study and work I did not gain such a mental spiritual uplift as in this one year of knowing and using Universal Life Energy. For this enlightenment I shall try to thank you by making your teachings practical in my own life, and I hope to assist others into the truth you have given to us so generously.

H. Stone
Retsil, WN. (WA)

Dear Mr. Fersen:

I heard of your work through a friend. I attended one of the lectures given at the Portland Hotel, and there I was invited to bring my children to the Junior classes.

There was such an improvement in my youngest child after attending these classes that my husband became interested and took the course. His health was very bad at that time and he was taking various medicines which did him no good at all. He took one treatment from one of the healers, and then took the course. Since taking the lessons and applying them to his daily life his health is so improved that we can scarcely believe it is true. His friends and the men where he works want to know what he has done to himself. He also has a better position, and has improved in all ways.

It has meant such a comfort to us since the children and my husband and I have learned to use the Life Force. We use it all the time for all things. Our medicine closet has been cleaned out, The Life Force has proved the best "first aid" I have ever found.

Since Mr. Tatlock has regained his health our home is so different that words will not tell it. We are a cheerful, happy family now.

Sincerely,
Mrs. C. Tatlock.
Portland, Oregon.

Dear Mr. Fersen:

Through the influence of my husband, I was led to take up the study of "Science Of Being" as taught and explained by you. Every lesson is a gem of precious worth.

More and more as time goes on I am realizing the teachings contained in these lessons. I am no longer searching for Truth. Truth is revealed to me now through the Conscious contact with it, as taught and explained in the lessons.

I have the very best of health and am able to meet and adjust my affairs in life without worry and anxiety, and am able now to help others in the same way.

Words can never express my gratitude for the wonderful revelations and realizations of the latent powers within, which I now am able to use consciously through the knowledge which this teaching brings. I have discovered that through "The Science Of Being," I can scientifically explain all I need to know – the how and why of things, that before seemed a mystery.

M. Atkins.
Los Angeles, Calif.
Pittsburgh, Ps., Sept. 16th 1924.

Dear Mr. Fersen:

I want to tell you what your teachings have given to me.

They have given to me the most valuable possession I ever had in my life; that is, a better understanding of that life, and an understanding with which I have made many changes in my life and in my mind.

I have lived more truthfully and more harmoniously since I became conscious of that which "The Science Of Being" has given to me.

It has given me enlightenment, which paves the way to peace and harmony and power.

I want to thank you for your kindness, patience and love.

You may use this if you care to.

Your thankful pupil,

In Light and with light,

J.F. Higgins.

Dear Mr. Fersen:

I am writing about my experience in treating according to your System.

One evening about six weeks ago, I dropped into a drug store for a dish of ice cream; while there, I was discussing the "Life Force" with the druggist, he being a doctor. He told me about a pain he had had in his back for over two years. He then suggested that I give him a treatment, which I did. In less than ten minutes he said the pain was gone. I asked him how he felt? He said it felt like an electric shock going down his spine, to the spot where the pain was and driving the pain away. He felt like an eighteen-year-old boy, his age being sixty years. He thought it was wonderful. He felt the vibrations all through his body.

I stopped in his store this evening to ask him how he felt; he said he was fine and dandy and the pain had never returned.

I could write a great many more. I have had very good success. THANKS to you for the WONDERFUL TEACHINGS.

L. Giltner
Bremerton, WN. (WA)

Dear Mr. Fersen:

It is with pleasure I am writing you in regard to my study of your teachings. I surely will never regret the time and money spent to obtain the lessons, and I am using the teachings every day in everything – work, business, and also a great deal in healing and helping others.

My quickest demonstration was a lady who came into my house to let me see how badly her eyes were swollen, and who asked for help, which I gave after making the contact with the Life Force. In less than ten minutes her eyes started to run pus. The swelling went down immediately and it was done so quickly that I myself could scarcely believe it was so.

Wishing you and yours all joy and success,

I remain,

B.A. Gillespie.

Bremerton, Wn. (WA)

Dear Mr. Fersen:

I have had the course in "The Science Of Being", and cannot express in words the good I have received. Before I took your course, Life to me was a closed book. But since taking it the book has been opened, and everything seems so clear and bright.

I am writing you these few lines to let the world know what these teachings did for me, knowing that they will do the same for anyone else.

G. Beyer.

Pittsburg, Pa.

To You Who Are Seeking Truth:

"The Science Of Being" was for me the A, B, C's which started an expansion of my consciousness that was being forced on me by Evolution.

My own application of the principles it teaches, in the use of Universal Life Energy for service to Humanity, has proven to me that it is not for only a chosen few but for everyone who chooses to serve unselfishly.

Written in words that can be comprehended by all who elect to learn, it opened the way to an understanding of many things which had puzzled me, dissatisfied as I was with blind acceptance on faith of "churched" teachings.

Sincerely,

H.W. Booth. Pueblo, Colo.

Section II:

Science Of Being Vibrations, Meditations & Exercises

"We do not find ideals in the material world.
We must find them in the Spiritual aspect of life."

~ Eugene Fersen

MEDITATION
"MANIFESTING ALL QUALITIES AND POWERS"

Written by Baron Eugene Fersen; best used when doing the Star Exercise or any other time when needed.

Thou art inspiring me on the Spiritual Plane.
Thou art guiding me on the Mental Plane.
Thou art sustaining me and protecting me on the Material Plane.
I am Thy individualized Projection into Thy own Eternal Substance Indissolubly connected with Thee Manifesting all Thy Qualities and Powers.

"BE MAN"—Express in every act of yours All ENERGY, INTELLIGENCE, TRUTH and LOVE; thus Living only will you live; thus acting only can you build to Freedom, Strength and Happiness in Life. This is your Problem: be this your Foremost Aim.

The Commandment of the Lightbearers

"VIBRATIONS"

Written by the Baron Eugene Fersen; used at meetings and teachings – these are the words written on the Lightbearer – The Morning Star picture.

SONS OF EARTH BROTHERS IN ETERNITY

SHAKE YOUR SOULS **AWAKE!**

THE HOUR SO LONG WAITED FOR, THE PROMISED HOUR HAS COME.

OVER THE DARK FIRMAMENT OF SUFFERING HUMANITY IS RISING THE

MORNING STAR.

HERALDING THE DAY WHEN YOU WILL UNDERSTAND AND THAT MAN'S

MOST SACRED DUTY IS TO BE MAN

THAT IS TO MANIFEST **LIFE, INTELLIGENCE, TRUTH AND LOVE**.

THERE IS NO HIGHER AIM NO VASTER PROBLEM

AND YOU REALIZING THIS

WILL BREAK THE FETTERS WITH WHICH IGNORANCE AND FEAR HAVE

BOUND UNCONSCIOUS HUMANITY

WILL STAND UP FREE

AND KNOW YOURSELVES TO BE THE ETERNAL MANIFESTATIONS OF THE UNMANIFEST

WITNESSES OF THE ABSOLUTE

SONS OF THAT GREAT ALL WHOM WE CALL **GOD**.

"VIBRATIONS"
Written by Baron Eugene Fersen and used at meetings and lectures

Father, I am Thy Individualized Projection into Thine Own Eternal substance proceeding from Thee, indissolubly connected with Thee, manifesting all Thy Qualities and Powers. I am indeed the image and likeness of Thee.

Mother, I am Thy Individualized Projection into Thine Own Eternal substance proceeding from Thee, indissolubly connected with Thee, manifesting all Thy Qualities and Powers. I am indeed the image and likeness of Thee.

Great Eternal One – The Creator of the Universe, I Thy created am Thy Individualized Projection into Thine Own Eternal substance proceeding from Thee, indissolubly connected with Thee, manifesting all Thy Qualities and Powers. I am indeed the image and likeness of Thee.

Divine Mother, Love Eternal, I Thy child am Thy Individualized Projection into Thine Own Eternal substance proceeding from Thee, indissolubly connected with Thee, manifesting all Thy Qualities and Powers. I am indeed the image and likeness of Thee.

And, as such, I am open on the physical plane to the influx of Divine Wisdom, Infinite Abundance and Limitless Supply. And on the Mental Plane my mind is open to the influx of Divine Wisdom and Thy Limitless Supply. And on the Plane of Spirit forever is my Soul open to the influx of Divine Wisdom, Eternal Love, and Limitless Supply. This realization comes down to the Mental Plane and on down to my everyday life where I KNOW I am open to influx of Divine Wisdom, Divine Abundance and Limitless Supply.

Father, Thou art inspiring me on the Spiritual Plane. Thou art guiding me on the mental plane. Thou art sustaining and protecting me on the physical plane.

The Mental Contact with Universal Life Energy
and
the Star Exercise

In order to contact Universal Life Energy mentally, relax as completely as you can, physically, mentally and emotionally. And, when you feel harmony within you as a result of that relaxation, then say aloud the following words: "I AM ONE WITH UNIVERSAL LIFE ENERGY. IT IS FLOWING THROUGH ME NOW. I FEEL IT." This statement can be repeated several times, but the important point is not the successive repetitions of it, but the realization of its meaning. The clearer the realization, the better the results. Thus, you open the mental door, which separated the life force within you from the Life Energy without. And, the force within, because of its inherent quality of Attraction, contacts the Force from without, which then begins to flow through you with an ever-increasing power, purifying and invigorating you all the time. The more you use that Force, the more it is supplied from the Infinite Source.

The "STAR EXERCISE," is indeed a "Key to All Power," as it unlocks and brings forth in Man all his latent powers and forces. It is when the human body takes the position as shown in the diagrams following that the actual contact of life energy within is made with the Universal Life Energy without. Stand straight, but relaxed, with legs spread at a degree corresponding to the design, the arms stretched to either side on a level with the shoulders, with head erect, and your body will fit into the five-pointed star. Even the proportions of a normally built body will correspond to the figure of the star. The head fits into the upper point, the two arms into the two side points, the torso into the center, and the legs into the two lower points. The palm of the left hand should be turned up, and that of the right down. The whole body must remain erect, but not tense. The palm of the left hand, turned up, draws in through its complicated network of nerves the Universal Energy present in the surrounding atmosphere, and the stream of Life Force pours into the body because of the attraction exercised on it by the inner life force of the body itself. Thus, is established a current of Universal Energy, penetrating from the Infinite Source into the human body, invigorating it and purifying it, and flowing out of it only to return with ever-increasing power. Not only through the left hand does the Life Force penetrate into the body; it pours in also through every cell, and very strongly through the solar plexus. Yet, during the exercise the main current is received as stated above. Shortly after having taken the position, you begin to feel a certain heaviness in the palm of the left hand. It is as if a heavy ball were pressing on the palm. And, one is sensible of a kind of tingling in the fingertips of the right hand. These two feel that the contact is established.

Here are a few more important points to be remembered in connection with this exercise. The best times to perform it are in the morning, immediately after getting up, before doing anything else, and at night, before going to bed.

Three to five minutes are all that is needed to perform the Star Exercise. For beginners, it would be inadvisable to do it longer, because of the very strong inflow of life forces. But later on, when the body becomes accustomed to that inflow of life currents, the duration of the Star Exercise can be prolonged to fifteen minutes, and the exercise taken more than twice a day. During that exercise, one ought to be dressed as lightly as possible, in order to leave the body free and without pressure on any part of it. The exercise should be performed in front of an open window, and never be taken immediately after a meal. At least an hour must elapse between the two; otherwise a nausea, and sometimes indigestion, may result, as the life current has the same effect on digestion as an electrical storm has on milk. It curdles the food in process of digestion, because of its strong chemical action. Deep, rhythmic breathing is very helpful in connection with the exercise, because of the stimulating effect of the oxygen. In the beginning, one's arms may feel tired in the performance of the exercise. No effort should be used to keep the arms up in their proper position. Let them drop, and lift them again when rested. Otherwise, the tension of the muscles and nerves resulting from a prolonged forced elevation of the arms will counteract, to a great extent, the flow of the Force through them.

The exercise works so automatically that there is no imperative need to think about the Force flowing through the body. It will flow anyway, because of the Law of Attraction.

The Star Exercise is exceedingly beneficial to children. It stimulates all of their bodies, especially their brain centers, and those glands which play such an important role in their growth and development.

FIVE-POINTED STAR

MAN WITHIN STAR

STAR EXERCISE

REJUVENATION EXERCISE

Sit quietly, relaxed in a chair with the left palm turned up on the left knee and the right palm turned down on the right knee. Enter into Silence and contact Universal Life Energy by the method previously explained. After you feel that Power flowing through your body – make the following statements in a low voice with eyes closed:

I am One with Universal Life Energy, which is flowing through me now, I feel it.

It is filling all the centers, cells, glands and organs of my body, my blood, my bones, my nerves and tissues; it stimulates them, rejuvenates them, strengthens them, harmonizes them.

I am One with Universal Life Energy, which is flowing through me now, I feel it.

It eliminates all my fears; it stimulates all my mental qualities; it develops my memory; it brings out and properly directs my will; it unfolds my intuition, it makes my thought strong, clear, creative; it makes me self-reliant.

I am One with Universal Life Energy, which is flowing through me now, I feel it.

It brings out all the priceless treasures of My Soul; it is the Power that heals, it is the Power that enlightens; it is the Power that makes me free; it is the Power that purifies and uplifts me; it brings me back my birthright, Harmony.

I am One with Universal Life Energy, which is flowing through me now, I feel it.

My life is a part of the Life of the Universe; my mind is a ray of the Supreme Intelligence; my sincerity is an expression of the Great Law, which is setting me free; my Love is a manifestation of the Universal Power of Attraction. Within my soul is shining the Soul of the Universe and now through Universal Life Energy, do I commune with Mother Nature, the Infinite One, the Source of all Being, Eternal and Harmonious.

N.B. These statements are not to be used as affirmations but must be mentally realized during their audible statement. From five to ten minutes should be the duration of the exercise. It is to be repeated every day if possible at the same hour and keep on until satisfactory results are obtained. Even then it is advisable to continue the exercise every day so as to hold the ground already obtained.

THE SPHERE
Taught to the Students and Lightbearer Members

When we put our hands together to form The Sphere, it is like holding the Light. This is seen in the picture of The Morning Star. This was not definitely planned. I unconsciously held my hands this way while posing, and did not notice it until I saw the painting. The Flame was intended to be a Light, but the artist saw it as a Star and painted it that way. She said, that as she looked at the Flame, it changed to the appearance of a Star. We thus have a painting of the Messenger carrying in the Sphere, a Star, the Morning Star.

When we make The Sphere, we have concentrated Light. Inside The Sphere is a rotary movement. The longer we hold The Sphere, the stronger the rotary movement becomes. Included in The Sphere is the Six-Pointed Star of Power, Abundance, Wisdom, Law, Harmony, and Protection.

The Sphere stimulates the Spiritual Self of the person whom we place in It. His stimulated Spiritual Self in turn stimulates his Life Center, and brings about a healing. After placing the person in The Sphere, we should think of Harmony. The realization of Harmony is not easy. We should just try to feel It.

There is the question whether one should place his own Spiritual Self in The Sphere in addition to that of the patient. The advantage is that one becomes more closely in contact with the patient. In doing so, place first oneself, saying "I am in The Sphere," then the name of the patient or problem. The disadvantage is that if one has not contacted the Eternal Power, one may take on the sickness temporarily of the patient. A good healer is usually successful in protecting himself from this.

The Sphere is the maximum concentration of Power so far known to us, provided we are in contact with the Eternal Power. If we are not in contact, The Sphere is only a concentration of human power, and anything negative can enter It.

Our **F**ather

Without beginning, without an End
Self-existent, Self-containing
Infinity Itself, Itself Eternity
Creating everything, Constituting everything
  Governing, Sustaining, Pervading and
  Containing everything
ONE from Whom all things originate and
  to Whom all things ultimately return
The LIFE of the Universe
Its Creative INTELLIGENCE
Its Governing LAW
Its Infinite LOVE and HARMONY
The SOURCE of all Beings, all Powers
  all Forces, all Laws, and their Fulfillment
Immovable in midst of Eternal Motion
Immutable in midst of Unceasing Changes
Substance of Matter
Essence of Spirit
This is our Eternal FATHER, the MOTHER
  of the Universe also, called NATURE by some
  and worshipped by others
  under the name of GOD.

                              THE LIGHTBEARER

18 November 1955

Copyrighted The Lightbearers 1956

Section III:

Original Public Lectures Announcements
&
Public Lectures by the Baron Eugene Fersen

"Science Of Being in Its completion, is our Higher Self."

~ Eugene Fersen

THE NEW ERA
OR
The Coming Order
Dawning now upon
MANKIND
How To Prepare ONESELF
For the Changing Standard
of LIFE
and
The World Crisis

Today's Events point out clearly that the Old Order of things is passing away to give place to a NEW ONE. Everything that Mankind has been holding as stable, reliable and sacred is crumbling now into dust and the whole Structure of Modern Civilization is shaken to its very Foundation.

Business, Political and Social Conditions, International Relations, Scientific Concepts and Religious Beliefs are tumbling down never to rise again in their present aspects, as the TIME FOR GREAT ADJUSTMENTS IS AT HAND NOW.

Never before in the History of Mankind have Human Beings had to face a Problem of such a Magnitude as the WORLD CRISIS of Today and, unless we prepare ourselves to meet it properly, we will not be able to stem the tide of Adverse Conditions and will be carried away by the great Flood of Disintegration which is now sweeping the World.

Men of great business ability, Politicians, Advanced Thinkers, Representatives of Religions, in fact Leaders of all branches of Modern Civilization, are suggesting all kinds of remedies to stop the ever rising tide of the Disintegration. Thus far their efforts have been in vain and will be so in the Future, because the Time has come when ordinary means cannot cope with extraordinary conditions. Something as great, in fact, Greater than the World Crisis of Today must be used in order to SOLVE THIS GREAT PROBLEM.

As it always has been in the Past that in Times of Great Human Distress something was given to Mankind to meet that Distress, there comes now a MESSAGE of such a magnitude that it can cope with the Present Day Condition. This MESSAGE is the SCIENCE OF LIFE ITSELF called SCIENCE OF BEING.

To carry properly that MESSAGE to all Nations, there was founded in 1921, in Washington, D.C., a worldwide Organization called THE LIGHTBEARERS, the definite Aim of which is to help Human Beings to meet successfully in their individual lives this World Crisis, which its founder already foresaw at that time.

Thousands have heard, or read, that MESSAGE and have come to realize that it is the very ONE that was prophesized 2000 years ago by Man's Greatest Friend, and confirmed by modern Seers such as Leo Tolstoy.

"THE MESSAGE"

called

"SCIENCE OF BEING"

(The Science of Living)

The Basic Aim of which is to LIBERATE Mankind from Ignorance, Superstition and Fear and INSURE to the Individual his Inalienable Birthrights of Freedom, Self-determination and Pursuit of Individual Happiness, thus MAKING LIFE WORTH LIVING.

SCIENCE OF BEING offers an up to date scientific explanation of "WHY" and "HOW" of human existence, an explanation that will satisfy that inner craving within each individual to know: Why he is born to this world? From where does he come and where does he go? What is his ultimate aim and purpose? Does life begin only with his human birth and end with his bodily death or is there a continuity of existence thereafter? Is life but a mere happening or is it directed by some definite Immutable Laws? Is there a Supreme Intelligent Power governing this Universe or is everything but a combination of Material Elements ruled by Hazard and Chance?

SCIENCE OF BEING teaches how to unfold, the Forces and Powers latent within the individual and use them daily in every department of human activities.

SCIENCE OF BEING builds CHARACTER and assures to everyone the realization of their Ambitions and Aims of Life.

SCIENCE OF BEING is a complete education in the Fine Art of Living, an art not taught in schools and colleges, yet without which nobody can get along through Life successfully.

The Explanation of the Science of Being Teachings?
by the Baron Eugene Fersen

Health, Success and Happiness are the Foundation and Aim of every human life. Health is Energy. It is your capital. The more you have of it, the better off you are.

Success, is the intelligent use to which you put your capital of Energy Health.

Happiness is the satisfaction you get from the proper combination of these two, Health and Success.

The Source of all Health, physical, mental and spiritual, is the limitless Life Energy of the Universe, from which all life in Nature springs. Every human being is equipped by Nature with the physical means to contact and use that Life Force. The more you contact it, the stronger and healthier you become, thus adding constantly to that initial capital of Energy of yours with which you have to make a Success in your life. Few have done so, because few have known that it could be done, and those few have kept the secret for themselves.

"Science of Being," simply strips the mystery and uncertainty from these plain, basic Truths of life and puts you in direct contact with Universal Forces and Laws amidst which you live. It teaches you to attune yourself intelligently to the gigantic ebb and flow of those Cosmic Currents, in such a fashion as to enlist their full power to help you reach your goal, instead of unconsciously opposing yourself to them.

Thus, it completely reorganizes your human existence from the bottom upwards, giving you first a sound physical body through which to express your activities, then a healthy and vigorous mind to govern and direct them most advantageously and finally a ready access to the priceless and unlimited soul treasures stored within you, as within every individual born to this world. You are started into a correlative growth and expansion on these three planes of your Being with results in corresponding material and intellectual rewards, not because those rewards are given to you from the outside, but because you have developed in yourself the strength of character and the ability to take them.

The majority of people today fumble blindly toward an end only vaguely seen, blundering awkwardly athwart the very Universal Laws and Powers that, properly handled, should be their greatest help. When they are flung back bruised and discomfited, they prey of ills physical, mental and spiritual, they sullenly place the blame on God, Fate, the local politician or anywhere except where it actually belongs – on their own ignorance.

"Science of Being," eliminates that guilty factor by giving you the right perspective of yourself in relation to the Universal Forces of which you are the product. It opens your eyes to the intangible elements with which you have to deal and delivers into your hands the conscious control of your own Destiny. You will know how to restore your bodily health when you are ill and how to increase your vitality and energy when you are well. You will develop your mental faculties to the highest degree. You will stabilize your emotional side, replacing fear by Confidence, nervousness by Poise and worry by Peace and Harmony.

Achievement is a prize locked securely inside that curious and delicate assortment of complex parts, which is YOU. All those parts need in order to pour forth into realization their measureless treasures of latent possibilities is the proper correlation one to another and to the Power which drives them. That is the end which it is the purpose of this Course to accomplish, so that you may be able, through the development of your own inherent qualities and forces, to experience to the full in this earthly existence the ultimate of all human desires – Health, Success and Happiness.

WHAT IS GOD?
Written by Baron Eugene Fersen

God is All Life, Intelligence, Law and Love. He is the Life which sustains the whole Universe, the Intelligence which guides the whole Universe, the Law which protects the whole Universe, and the Love which holds together everything in a sense of Harmony.

The Father of the Universe is the One who Creates, Constitutes, Governs, Sustains and contains All. The word God does not mean anything to a person unless he has a preconceived idea of it. The Masons called God, the Great Architect, the Great Builder.

It is difficult in present world conditions to believe there is a God. Yet we must believe that the fundamental Principle of Life exists. Plants in the Spring are regenerated. Science has proven there is energy, and energy is Life. Everything in the Universe pulsates, or moves, and that is Life. Life is a word coined by us to explain the functioning of energy. Energy is the foundation of life, and is Life. No one can deny there is an extraordinary Intelligence, which has constituted everything in its place. No one can deny, even in this lawless community which we call Humanity, that Law does not exist. Laws cannot be abolished. We have to recognize them. All evil in this world is due to violation of Laws. This violation causes friction, and in friction there is always loss. Proper working of Laws has no friction. Laws still work, but we are not in tune with them. The Power which we call Love is sustaining us, holding us together. Remove the Power from our body, and the body dies. Remove It from our heart and we become cold, hard-hearted.

We cannot explain the Unexplainable in a way. We must approach It from all sides. The concept of God is so colossal that our human mind can only touch a fraction of it. The word Infinity means no end. Modern people are so sophisticated, so complicated, that they want complicated answers. The simplest things are usually the greatest.

No Being, no Spirit will ever understand Infinity and Eternity. Only Infinity KNOWS Itself, and Infinity is God. Also Eternity is God. If we were to finally grasp God, then we would merge with God. Through the whole of Eternity, we will always be exploring God, and learning more of It. This will always be very interesting.

What is Science?
Written by Baron Eugene Fersen

Webster defines Science as organized knowledge. That is the best definition of science. When knowledge is not organized, it is not science.

When a bird builds a nest, it uses its Higher Self to build the nest where it should be and how it should be. The bird uses knowledge, but it cannot really be called science, because the bird is not consciously aware of doing it this way. The Superconsciousness in plants awakens in the seed the stimulus to grow. Subconsciousness in anything does not want it to grow.

Science is that knowledge which we feel is correct and organized. Science of Being means organized knowledge of existence. It includes the Four Square Principle, including Spirit and Its counterpart Matter. When we live in the Four Square, we are both spiritual and material, successful on the physical, mental and emotional planes.

Eternal existence is already organized, completed from Eternity. The Eternal cannot add anything to It. It will never be completely revealed to us. This will furnish the interest, stimulus and variety of living. Only the Eternal KNOWS ALL. It broadens Itself through us, greater and greater in every direction.

Science of Being is the perfect understanding of everything. We will never be able to learn today what we should learn tomorrow. If we could, there would be a missing link. If there were a missing link, it would be disorganized. Human science is in almost all cases, very inaccurate. Mathematics is probably the exception.

The whole Universe is based on science, and science is the Four Square. If we do anything the Four Square way, we do it scientifically.

We cannot improve our Higher Self. We can give It the opportunity to express Itself. Our Higher Self Knows All that God Knows, and has known all throughout all Eternity. It is not The All, but a Ray of All. It will never come to the end of knowing Itself. It will always be progressing. This is very difficult for the human mind to understand. There will always be an increased feeling of expanding inside. "Know Thyself and Thou Shalt Know All."

DEMOCRACY AND THE LAND OF FREEDOM
Lecture by the Baron Eugene Fersen

With all this talk for Democracy, and Freedom, I often wonder if the average individual knows what he or she is talking about? And, if they really think this war, at home and abroad, is being fought to accomplish this very thing? I wonder if they think that just buying war bonds, and giving money to the Red Cross, sending money to China, and feeling very Patriotic, will win this war for Freedom and Democracy?

There is no evidence of this sort of feeling expressed in any way on a large scale, so how much would you say exists in a small way? Say among individual groups? Do you know of any religious body, which expresses within itself this feeling of Freedom and Democracy? Would you say that even fifty percent of any religious body would share within their home, the Joys and Sorrows of any being, regardless of race, color, or religious belief, providing that they were clean, polite and friendly? That I point out the religious groups is because that is the place where tolerance, justice, and love are supposed to be taught. If it has been taught the teachings have gone astray, have been to no avail, because it is just not being lived.

Does it stand to reason that if these things are not lived among smaller groups, that it could be lived among the peoples of the world? So, why all this talk about post- war plans, when the war is not won yet? Or will be won, until the peoples of the world live among themselves a living Democracy, and a living Freedom?

I will take you to a still smaller group, the Family. Does Democracy exist in the average Family? Is Mother accorded the same freedom even by Law, that which is accorded to Father? Women's Rights, for instance? If Democracy were being lived within the home, would there be such a movement as "Rights for Women"? There are many instances where men do not exercise the rights that are given to them by human law, because they are intelligent enough to know that to do so would disrupt the harmony of home.

How can we be considered the supposed Great Democracy of the world, when it is the husband's rights, by man made laws to have the whole say, as to how and when and where, the money of a family unit should be used? There are men that do not take advantage of this law, because of its unfairness. Within a family unit, where this law is taken advantage of, there is no democracy and the unit as a whole has been subjected to Totalitarian Rule. They are held down by economic reasons, not lifted up, by democratic rule, which is based on Equality. How many families would you say are ruled by democracy, or totalitarian methods? Right here in the United States of America, in our own American homes?

Now, I will take you to a still smaller unit, the individual. Every living being is at war within them. Where is the Peace? Where is the Freedom? If you think you are not at war within yourself, you are only asleep, because the being that is not at war within themselves is Four Square, and to be Four Square is an achievement that few beings have reached. What does it mean to be Four Square?

The outward manifestation of the living Four Square is – Health, physical and mental, Strength, physical and mental, Happiness, physical and mental, and Freedom, physical and mental. If you have all these things, the Spiritual Quality of you will express itself in such beauty that all who come near you will stand in awe. If you would like to reach this state of being, the Four Square Principle can guide you to it. If you would like to be democratic, The Four Square Principle can guide you to it. If you would like to be free, The Four Square Principle can guide you to it. Here is the formula:

"Express in every act of yours ALL ENERGY, INTELLIGENCE, TRUTH AND LOVE," thus acting can you build to Freedom, Strength, and Happiness in Life. This is your Problem; be this your Foremost Aim.

This is the formula; it means just what it says, no more, no less. It is to be used, to only think about it gives the same result as the ingredients of a cake. Until you have put them together, there is no cake.

Now let's retrace our steps back to the beginning. The individual unit has tried to make democracy work, this spreads his influence into the family, the family spreads its influence into the group, the group spreads its influence into the nation, and the nation spreads its influence into the world. When this happens, we could really begin talking about Democracy and Freedom, in a post-war world. To think it may be accomplished in any other way is only blindness, because there is not one thing in Nature that grows from the outside in. All things grow from the inside out. Man has tried so hard to make it work the other way, and because he will not see, his problems keep getting worse all the time.

They try to straighten the tangles by trying just a little bit harder to make it work from the outside. This is what they are trying to do now, with such energy, using all the intelligence and wit they can muster together to out think the other fellow, but there is no Truth, and certainly no Love. Millions of young lives will be lost, their wits strained to the nth degree, because they have forgotten what they are fighting for.

When they are all exhausted, I wonder if they will wonder what they started fighting for in the first place? How did it stray so far from the Principle aim? It is simple, they just planted the wrong seed; instead of planting democracy they planted greed; and when their victory garden sprouts a monster instead of a Democracy, they will start fighting the monster. It takes so much energy to fight a monster, and if the victory is ours, what has been accomplished? When we have him lying at our feet, we still have to start all over again, and plant a new seed; will we know which seed is Democracy next time? Or, will we choose another monster?

Of course we want Freedom; it is our natural inheritance, but WE must do something about it. Don't let the thought that you cannot do it because you have no say in the matter, put you back into a state of lethargy. There is no Ruler in the whole world, that can tell you what to think, maybe there is one who can tell you what to do, but it is your Freedom to think, as you will. WE cannot stop another from thinking what they will, neither can they stop us from thinking what we will, unless we let them think for us. And, right thinking plants the seed for good.

No, it will not be done in a day, or month, or even years, but YOUR thinking will bring to you, either a monster or a democracy, which do you want to create?

LIFE AS I SEE IT
Lecture by Baron Eugene Fersen

We are born, we marry, we procreate, and we die…Why? We all ask ourselves this question. The old belief that those things should remain a mystery, some how does not satisfy us any more. What's more it should not, because mystery is symbolic of ignorance, and it is man's duty as man to claim his inheritance given by Divine right to express the image and likeness of the Creator. We are the highest form of life on earth, and as such, should know why and what we are here for, nor were we meant to be blind, but to be alert, aware, and to live life to its fullest. All of life is based on the law of analogy, as it is on a small scale, so it is on the largest scale. The same law rules everything, from the smallest electron, to the largest planet. I am sure there must be a reason for living, therefore, I will, to the best of my ability try to give you my version of the beginning and the end, of which there is no beginning and no end. Just a sphere, how we gain entrance into this world, and where we go, when we leave it.

In order to help you understand the beginning; I will explain a few facts. As you know, Science has proven that all of life is vibration. Different rates of vibration determine the difference in the substance of different objects such as the human body, which carries a different rate of vibration than does the rock. And, we are all vibrating within the vibration of the Universe. The human body is manifesting on three planes - Physical, Mental and Emotional, that is why we are called a Triune being. We each have our own rate of vibration, and no two individuals are alike. So, when the male and female procreate, at the very moment of conception, they draw to themselves a soul, of like vibration. This is the soul's way of entrance into a physical world. To say we did not ask to come into this world is not so. We seek out our own parents, like attracts like, and so we begin life on earth by being born.

*

The first seven years of life is devoted to getting used to our environment, good or bad, therefore our environment is a combination of our own rate of vibration. If this one phase alone were understood, our lives would be much more understandable. The parents would seek to learn from the child, and the child would learn more readily from the parents. Each character trait carries its own pattern for this life. That is why it is so foolish for the parents to tell the child one thing, then do the opposite, because the child will take on the character traits through vibration before it can understand words. We can pretend with words, but not with vibrations.

1933 WINTER COURSE IN THE SCIENCE OF BEING

First Lesson: Tuesday, December 19th, 1933

Given at the Lightbearers' Auditorium, Montreal, Canada

By Baron Eugene Fersen

THE PURPOSE AND AIM OF LIFE

We have been together many times to take various lessons in the Science of Being, but I know that this time the purpose of our coming together is different. We are not only anxious to know something more about living, but we wish information on what we shall have to face.

From any angle we take it today, Life is so complex and vast that it would take an eternity to grasp it as a whole. This condition should not appall us because if we were able to grasp it all, and there was nothing more to understand or to strive for, we would stagnate. So, there must always be a next step for us to take, and the mere fact that there is a next step, stimulates us.

You all realize that the times in which we live are different from anything we have ever experienced before, no matter how long anyone has lived.

In the memory of most of us is the World War, but even that tremendous upheaval cannot compare with the events unfolding before us in these days in which we live. While in those war days there was evidence of a peculiar restlessness, still it was unlike the unrest of today. The reason for this difference in feeling between then and now is that we are facing something unique. It is as if we were passing over a threshold from one room to another; whenever we cross any threshold there is a change. We must prepare ourselves for that change. The strange thing about it is that although signs and portents foreshadow change clearly, almost the totality of humanity completely ignores it.

Human beings deliberately close their eyes to it; they do not want to see it. It would appear as if some evil force blinds them. But, there are no evil forces in the generally accepted meaning of that word. There is only that which is good and that which is not good, that which is constructive and that which is destructive.

The reason why such conditions seem like an evil force, blinding us at a time when we most require our mental and spiritual sight to be clear, is because of the operation of the Law of Polarity. The Law of Polarity always works and in this instance, in the following way:

The coming changes being so tremendously powerful produce different rates of vibration new to both mind and soul, and to some extent to our bodies. If we lived according to natural Law, humanity would be so relaxed that they would not be so upset; they would offer no resistance. They would accept it and it would enter them; if the thing were good they would embrace it, if not, they would eliminate it. This would be a great difference from our present attitude. We usually accept or reject a thing with our limited human discrimination. We can only discriminate from the angle we gaze from. If the angle is wrong or narrow, then the result will be wrong. That is why in most cases human judgement and opinion are so faulty, one cannot blame them for they can do no more than analyze a question from their own perspective.

To change this angle they must first accept the new idea mentally before it becomes valuable to them. Their failure to do so produces undesirable effects because the cause was undesirable. Often when we think we exercise discrimination, we are merely using premises as facts, we make our own facts to suit our desires, and this mental blindness causes us perhaps to reject something of value.

If we were relaxed there would be a continuous flow of vibrations from the outside into us with the possibility of becoming receptive to thoughts on all three planes which would be constructive for us, and which now we are incapable of assimilating. For instance, those who do not know about dietetics use food wrongly, thus good food becomes destructive; we thus live in a fool's paradise.

As it is on the physical plane, so it is on the mental. We make mistakes unknowingly, but the Law excuses no failure. It knows what is good for us, so all we need to do is let the Law help us.

All is vibration. Even when we eat, vibration is the dominant keynote. Anything, which the eyes can see, vibrates. When the mind perceives, it is by the means of vibrations. When one perceives the thoughts of others, it is again through the vibrations called telepathy. With the Spiritual, it is the same. The vibrations of Spirit are Life itself. That is why vibrations are so tremendously important and so fundamental to everyone on the physical, mental, and spiritual planes. There is not a place where they are not. Life itself vibrates and Life, remember, is a closed cycle. We as human beings cannot understand the Infinity of Time and Space. There is no use for us to try to understand, but we can use our imagination to picture Life as a closed cycle. It starts at a given point, goes around in cycles and returns to its starting point. We are the visible, condensed crystallization of Life, therefore, the very foundation of our three-fold nature is Life Vibrations.

Life cannot go against itself for the simple reason that it cannot turn against itself, as it is itself. Life cannot reverse the hands of time; it cannot therefore, reverse itself.

The condition of no Life, we call death. If Life turned against itself there would be produced a state of absolute death. The death of animals, plants, minerals, even of gases, but of people it is not really death; it is transition. Death and annihilation, does not exist. Vibrations are indestructible; death has no power over them.

Life, therefore, not being able to turn against itself, carries its own vibrations through its own channels and always produces constructive results, for if a vibration is undesirable for an individual, the individual eliminates it just as the physical body gets rid of undesirable conditions through natural detoxification processes.

There is a continual process of elimination going on in all three Planes, and if we human beings would only be open-minded, which is better than being broad-minded, all we would get would be constructive – even negative vibrations, though they entered us, would not harm us. When new thoughts enter and harm us, it is because there is an opposition to their passage. The less opposition there is, the greater results are obtained. Thus, we have humanity facing incoming vibrations of all sorts and opposing them at all stages of their rhythm.

Rhythm is in all things. Consider the very latest discoveries in regards to light. Light has been considered an immovable yardstick in the Universe. Its speed was established at one hundred eighty six thousand and a few hundred miles per second, but now as a result of experiments by Professor Mickelson and his successors, it has been discovered that the speed of light varies to the extent of twelve miles per second. Furthermore, it varies in a rhythmic way according to the time of day and the season of the year. There is an ebb and flow. The entire scientific world is puzzled, but some day they will see that there is nothing to be puzzled about – it is all according to the Law of Rhythm, which is manifest everywhere.

So today, we have on account of that same Law of Rhythm, a new cycle. We must, therefore, be open-minded and not offer any resistance to its emergence. This does not mean that we must be carried along by others' thoughts. On the contrary, we must try to think for ourselves and not follow the masses. Today, there is more danger than ever in following the masses.

As it has ever been, only the few individuals are right. You know the popular say, "Vox Populi, Vox Dei," (The voice of the people [is] the voice of God,) but if any phrase is wrong, it is this one. The fact that masses are wrong can be clearly seen when we realize that masses as a whole have extremely closed minds. In every way they are tense, therefore, closed to outside influence. They offer greater obstruction as a group than the individual component to the vibrations traversing them. Consider several countries where the will of the few has been imposed on the many. Think for how long those who wished to impose their will on the masses tried but did not succeed.

According to our perception, Life appears to us bigger and better, and if we are to get out of it all that it has for us, we must approach it with expansive perception and an even bigger acceptance. For to perceive, is not alone sufficient. You must take it in so that it becomes a part of you and you of it, and the fact that we meet so much opposition in doing so, proves that it has its use.

Let us now consider Time in this connection. With us a year is a year, with Life there is all Eternity. We cannot approach Life from a limited point of view; we must take it from the Absolute point of view.

Consider the relative length of certain periods in Life. Strange as it may appear those periods, even years, are not of equal duration. Time is not necessarily measured by the revolution of the earth around the sun. It is gauged by our perception. If we perceive it in a certain way, it appears long; if in another way, a year can be but a day. These things show that our limited methods of measuring time have a relative value. When we come to certain crucial moments, the top speeds in the life of humanity, time appears to speed up.

Even in our individual lives this is true. Consider when we were children how slowly time went by and how much one could put into a few minutes. On the other hand, the moment we are grown up, think how little we can do in five minutes. The above is due to the fact that we have reduced space and time in our own mind by increasing its speed. If we could cross from one end of Infinity to another in the twinkling of an eye, we could reduce Infinity to a point. The same would occur with Eternity. It would become a flash, but in that flash you would get the maximum power; in any event there would be no loss of Power whether spread out or centralized.

Thus, it is with human beings when they reach the maximum of their lives – their attitude toward time and space changes. Time seems quicker and space shorter, and in reality it is so.

If you could get outside our planet and see it from a point far enough away, you would see an increase in speed and a shortening of time compared to previous periods. Today things come swiftly upon each other, and as we are confronted continually by them we lose the proper power to comprehend, and the swift bombardment of events causes numbness. Today, because humanity is being hit with such a rapid succession of events, they have become numb, and once numbed they are blind, whereas if they had the power to resist it would stimulate them. There are a few who are stimulated by all the tremendous happenings around them, they become keener of perception, but they are exceptions, and the dominant fact among the vast majority is that they become numb.

When this happens, the Law of survival of the fittest strikes them out as unfit to take the next step. They are then automatically eliminated by that Law, because being numb, they make mistakes that bring them to destruction (not annihilation). When I say the masses, I include also the representatives of the masses. Those in power who stand as icons for mass feeling. They are not individual, but samples of their group with all the characteristics of the groups concentrated in them.

Consider a pear and its stem – the stem although different from the pear and seemingly a connecting link, nevertheless has all the chemical units that are found in the fruit; you could make a pear out of the stem, and vice versa. The pear is the top of the stem and the stem connects it with the branches of a tree. In the same manner, heads of government have the same mental and emotional core as the masses they stand for, and like the stem of our simile, they are in concentrated form.

Consider the teachings of Jesus. They were great teachings and yet at the same time they were not perceived and accepted by the majority around him. It is like standing too close to a huge rock or a large mountain. One never realizes what a tremendous thing it is, but the further away one is, the more its greatness is seen. Think to yourself what brings out the most in crowds, a football game or a lecture on world events, and your answer will be – the game. This is natural because although the game is of small importance for by merely watching it you can see it. A game can never be of importance in human life – it produces merely relative development, yet such games appear to loom large because they are small.

The reverse is true when we come to big things; we fail to give them their proper perspective. We see merely the part which the extents of our vision permits, and yet, if that same event were far enough away in time or space from us, even those of narrow vision would see it. At the moment it happens, it can only be appreciated by those with the broadest vision. For this reason, although we are living today in a period when each day is a page of momentous history, we fail as a whole to grasp its tremendous importance. Nevertheless, we are led step by step towards a crowning event; broad or narrow-minded alike, will be forced to take notice.

It is like people who walk on a cobblestone street wrapped in a daydream; they fail to notice the cobbles until they step on a really large one. This is what is going to happen to the majority of people in a comparatively short time. They will get the surprise of their lives, and they will blame everyone. Whereas, if they would only wake up and look around them, taking precautions to avoid the downward rush, preparation for a later ascent, they would be more equipped for that climb. We are supposed to know a little more than the crowds, and should do the best we can to prepare ourselves for the life that we will have to live in the near future.

This evening before coming to the Class, we speculated on how many new students would be present. I gave a figure which I was absolutely sure would be right. I said none would come, and although we have some students not belonging to Montreal, still no new students came despite our last night's audience, which was an intelligent one and in a way a receptive one. Why was this? Because as I explained, they represent the masses and the masses represent opposition to those things that would, if adopted, mean balance in their lives, but because they are numb and not stimulated by the extraordinary events we experience daily, they cannot perceive this. However, we will do the best in this class for everyone, not only for the students but for those without, for the time will come when they will call for help and we must be prepared to extend it.

1933 WINTER COURSE IN THE SCIENCE OF BEING

Second Lesson: Wednesday, December 20th, 1933

Given at Lightbearers' Auditorium, Montreal, Canada

by Baron Eugene Fersen

CREATIVE URGE

Of all the important things for us to consider, the most important is Life because without Life we could not exist. Therefore, the study of Life is the most important thing for every human being. Some may say that humanity studies everything which is related to Life, but Life itself as a fundamental study is hardly ever studied because they do not know how to live. And, as long as human beings will not understand the fundamental principles of Life and live accordingly, life cannot be and never will be worth living. All the trouble which humanity suffers and will continue to suffer is entirely due to their lack of knowledge of Life.

In order to study the principles of Life, we must first start by asking, "What is the aim of Life?" Not only one's individual life, but the aim as taken from the broadest angle, the sum total of Life. What, therefore, is the aim of Universal Life? It can be summarized in the following statement: "The aim of all Life is to persevere in its existence through the continuity of successive unfoldment." It is called the Law of Progress.

Let us analyze the above statement. There is a unit, which although intangible is nevertheless substantiated by facts – these facts all around us show us that Life's main aim is to continue to express itself, to persevere in its existence. In other words, to remain forever Life, that is its main aim. Life must be true to itself, which means to do the utmost to Live. This is shown by the Four Square, which is the foundation of our teachings.

As you all know, in that Square - the first corner is Life, the second is Mind, the third is Truth, and the fourth is Love. What, therefore, does Life face? It faces Truth. In other words, it must be true to its own nature, to persevere in its existence.

For the above reason, everything in nature, not only human beings, but animals, plants, even minerals and gases have implanted in them that fundamental trait to cling to existence, to hope against hope, to fight against all opposition, to stick to life.

In human beings this tenacity to Life is their most powerful trait; among plants likewise, for before they die they do their utmost to live. Before minerals dissolve, they do their utmost to hold together; before gases disintegrate they also do all they can to remain a unit. All this is the fight for existence.

Energy is the product, the manifestation of Life. We are the children of Life; therefore the fundamental trait of Life must be to express. That is why to kill is one of the most unnatural things, for it goes against the fundamental principle of life, which says, "Thou shalt Live!"

That is the Commandment – there is no other. The one, "Thou shalt not kill," is only there because of human ignorance, and when people will know and understand the Aim of Life, killing will cease, not only killing of human beings, but also killing in general. The killing of animals is bad, in a lesser degree, so is the killing of trees and of minerals and gases. There should be no killing on this planet.

You may point out that the whole of modern life is based on killing. That is what is wrong with human concepts, for if Life were based on killing, it would end by killing off its own existence and end in extinction; yet Life can only persevere through the continuity of successive unfoldment. In this statement is the whole wisdom and beauty of Life.

What does the above mean? A thing, which continues has no end. Continuity does not admit any end – it is endless. In other words, Life is Eternal. What is successive unfoldment? It means every step is a step in advance, a broader, deeper step, shaping itself like a fan, boundless, and limitless. Infinity and Eternity being the limit of Life's unfoldment, and as there is no end to Infinity and Eternity, so unfoldment is endless. How different this is from our conception of Life. If Life were accepted as a limitation it would become boresome and we would welcome extinction. Life is only desirable when we can say – "Today is greater than yesterday and tomorrow will be greater than today."

You may ask, "Can this be proved? Does life actually grow through successive unfoldment?" We can prove that is so by observing that everything possesses this capacity. Plants grow, animals grow, and we grow. True, when we reach a certain point, we stop, but this is due to a violation of the Laws of Life and is not in obedience to them.

If we were in tune with Life we would continue to grow, just as among certain Indian tribes in Mexico were found men of the age of ninety who can out run a deer by tiring it out.

Instead of shrinking with age, those men actually grow in stature. The same thing is found among animals; almost to their end they grow and when they stop growing they rapidly disintegrate and die. They hardly know anything of old age. Human beings are but animals of a high standard of mentality – all the chemicals and principles in them are the same; their growth obeys the same laws as govern plants, yet because of human ignorance and stubbornness no progress is made.

Stubbornness is not will power; it is a sign of ignorance, for humanity as a whole is a stubborn animal. We talk of mules, yet they are far below human beings in stubbornness. Human beings could be otherwise, but their own stubbornness interferes with their unfoldment.

Returning to our consideration of Life as a continuous unfoldment, you may doubt the accuracy of my statements, so I will approach it from another angle, that of pure mathematics. Of all sciences, mathematics is supposed to be the most exact. For this reason it is at the foundation of all other sciences. No matter what direction you turn, you cannot do without mathematics.

Mathematics, therefore, proves the statement I made that Life perseveres in its existence through continual unfoldment. Take this example: If we had only number 1, it would not progress. Mathematics is not thereby satisfied – it demands unfoldment to 2, and from 2 to 3, and 3 to 4 and so on. When we come to the end of the signs, or 9, we start all over again – 1 with 0, 1 with 1, etc. There is again a continuity of a very imperfect nature, imperfect because human beings have not imagined beyond 9. Why should 10 be two digits? It could be one figure, and we should be able to reach no end of figures. Probably mental laziness causes us to go on and on, and as we unfolded new symbols, our ability to do so would grow. Still returning to what we have achieved in that direction, we see that each step is an unfoldment, and one could calculate for all Eternity and still continue to count, for each time you take a successive step you have to advance to a bigger figure.

Thus it is with Life. If you want to take a successive step it has to be in growth. In the above we have the expression of Life, or the aim of its principle, as concisely and as clearly as it is possible to express it. Probably later we shall see it more clearly, because the more we live the clearer our vision becomes and the stronger the perception. But, today the mathematical analogy answers clearly the question – "What is the aim of Life?"

An understanding of this would do away with the blind questions, "What is the purpose of life? Why was I born?" When people will understand the purpose of Life, they will never ask that question and though you may not be aware of it, that question has been asked by some of the greatest thinkers on earth.

How can Life achieve that aim and purpose which I have just explained? It can do so by a fundamental trait or quality, which it possesses – the quality to create. With that fundamental trait, everything in Life is endowed either as creation or procreation, although the latter is secondary to creation. It is always thus for the word that is simple is the biggest and the additions are side issues. Procreation is a side issue of creation. Through the quality of creation, Life is able to multiply itself without an end, nor can it ever have an end because each step becomes a basis for further unfoldment.

Again, we see this in mathematics. Naturally, as numbers are not living they cannot create the thing themselves – they require a human mind or an outside Power to help them. We could call this process Procreation as it fits the case better than Creation, for when one is added to one you obtain two – that is Procreation – it is an addition from the outside.

There are other ways of procreating in mathematics, by multiplication for instance. In multiplication the numbers are in a different relation – they are not only close together, but they penetrate each other, and their complete combination we call multiplication. Multiplication is a combination from every angle; addition is a combination from one angle. In multiplication you put the figure all over the other and get a larger figure. This is Procreation.

In every department of Life we see Creation and Procreation. That is how Life is able to continue its existence throughout Eternity – it multiples. We human beings think that the multiplication of ourselves by Procreation is most important, but this is not at all so.

The way Life is achieved is through Creation; that is why we are so endowed and in that endowment is included the power of procreation, but in a way, it is the least of our creative powers. The greatest power which either mortals or immortals possess is the power to create. That is why a child likes to do something. It is a divine quality, the greatest there is, but think how little the average person uses it. Consider our modern life, what do we create? Hardly anything…We find it too much trouble.

Do you realized that the natives of Central America are much more advanced than we are because they take pains to create all sorts of things, but we go to the store and buy them. Even there we fail to use our creative power, half the time those who enter a shop don't know what they want to buy. I went shopping today and watched the people buying. It is an education to see how little they know of what they want, such people are sterile. It is a sign of complete mental sterility to accept thoughts of others without thinking. I prefer to give it its true name – Modern Sterilization.

Nor can we point to all that has been created and which we use unthinkingly in our modern lives. These things belong to but a few individuals – the rest take advantage of them. It is like adopting the children of someone else. This is a very important point for it is one of the greatest drawbacks of civilization, which though containing much good, is turned negative by so much of what is not good.

All this is hard to explain properly until we know the Law of Progress, which says, "Life perseveres in its own expression through continuity of successive unfoldment." When we understand and use this Law we can say truthfully that the good is greater than the evil, and there is progress.

It is like a mathematical problem – no matter how human beings violate the principles – they cannot pervert them because the principle is greater than its expression. Therefore, the principle always rules through us and consequently the principle with its laws is greater than the whole of mankind, and the statement that civilization advances in spite of mankind, is true.

How can we exercise these creative powers of ours? Let us first ask - How can we discover them? Most human beings have not the faintest idea that they have creative powers. They believe that they can only become copyists and imitators, but as long as one is an imitation, one cannot be one's self. You cannot even start to be what Life meant you to be while you have such a standard.

Such a false standard is destructive to human character because it prevents not only the exercise, but also the discovery of one's own creative powers. We cannot create by proxy, but we can by doing the work by ourselves, putting creative effort into it. Remember Life does not work by proxy – it demands immediate attention.

I will not give you a way by which I believe you will discover more creative power within yourself than you ever suspected; however, you can test it out for yourself. There is no use to say you have no time, although it will require a lot of mental digging, as far back as you can remember, and that will not be accomplished in one sitting. Try to go back successively through the whole of your Life. Don't start with the beginning – take the latest memories first for that will bring back events more clearly because it is in accordance with definite mental laws.

When you have understood the process, start analyzing your daily life in your relation to others and to life. Then try to extract the nuggets of gold in your life – that is the creative acts or thoughts you may have had. What have you actually created? Do you know that you will be surprised at the scarcity of such acts in your life?

You will find plenty of movement in your life – like the crisscrossing of fishes in an aquarium, darting hither and thither, but you will find few creative acts. Seek something that you have actually created, and you will be surprised by how little you have created. Why…Because some have disregarded that fundamental quality of creation.

You must analyze your life and you will see that the younger you get, as you look backward, the more creative you were. This is true of the majority, but some become creators later in life, and the rest take advantage of the work of others, failing even to give the real creators proper credit. This lack of gratitude is again because of their lack of creative power, for gratitude is a form of creation since it is an extension of ourselves, and an extension of anything involves creative power.

We commemorate at this Christmas time the birth of one who created; one who gave his very vivid and real life in order to awaken his fellow beings from their sleep of death. Yet, those who are supposed to commemorate the birth of that man Jesus, merely make a holiday of it and have a "good time," and expect more presents than they give. In all this there is nothing creative, just acceptance. Naturally there are exceptions to this, but I speak of the attitude of the majority.

Going back to the experiment I suggested that you make, when you reach back into the period of childhood and recall even trivial things, remember how important they were to your whole being. Live again in your childish creative triumphs; observe what will happen. Now that you will have the understanding, Life will be awakened within you, the blinders will be removed from your eyes and you will for the first time begin to feel a resurgence of the creative urge within you.

You won't be able to help this, for memories of creative urges of the past years are still alive in you. In recalling them you will recollect not a dead urge but a live one, and because you have advanced in understanding you will feel it like a force to set you on fire. You may even get an explosion, but never mind, better an explosion than to be dormant. There is nothing worse than to be living dead.

It is not easy to regain lost efficiency, it cannot be achieved overnight, but if you will persevere the reward will be far beyond your expectations. I have tried it and it succeeded. I could not have lived through the difficulties – physical, mental and emotional, which have come into my life during the last few years unless I had had that extraordinary creative urge. It is the only thing that keeps me alive.

You all know how close I was to the "beyond" when I was with you last year. Compared to then I am much stronger physically and in every other way. The mere fact that I survived is due to that creative urge which I awoke by the very method I have just explained to you.

There is another thing I want to tell you. We must take into consideration the requirements of life and the requirements of Life are the following: First of all, Life wants everyone to be free – no good work can be achieved unless we are free. Nature guarantees us individual freedom in order to preserve the creative urge. Freedom is not license; it is cooperation and coordination. It means to be able to use all one's powers in the most constructive way with no one behind us to force us. Our intelligence should lead us to do the right thing, a right action liberates, and mistakes entangle us.

To gain the greatest freedom we must try to do the best in life, that is the first condition, it is our birthright to success in life.

Next, comes self-reliance. We cannot be free if we rely or lean on someone. When we analyze life we find that the lesson of self-reliance is always taught. Take animals, especially birds. The bird in the nest is taken care of to the minutest detail, far beyond what human beings can do for their young. As long as they have not reached the flying stage, their parents meet every need, but when the parents feel that they are ready for independence, though the young birds themselves don't realize it, the parents teach them individually.

Consider a bird enticing its young from the nest with food held beyond its reach. It is pitiful how few human beings do the same with their children. Some parents never let their children grow up, some throw them like little featherless birds out of the nest because they, "haven't the means." There is no such thing as a mother or father bird not having the means. They will die first. Of how many human beings can the same be said? Parents, who act thus, violate a fundamental law, which even a crow respects.

It is said that children should earn money when young. They therefore, consider money the primary and all the child's primary viewpoint is directed to money. Such children come to value human beings by the amount of money they possess. Parents should give everything to their children and bring them to the point of independence. This does not mean to give in to their every whim.

It is very easy to procreate a child, but out of that procreated child, the parent has to create a being, build something beautiful, something strong of it, and if the parents do not fulfill that duty they are not worthy of the name.

Self-reliance is one of the things which humanity needs above all others, yet they do not know how to evoke it in their own children. Children should be taught self-reliance. There are organizations that greatly advance the teaching of self-reliance of children. To do a good deed a day, thus utilizing one's creative power in the best way. It is not like paying someone to do something. Consider the nightingale, it sings not because it is paid, but because it enjoys it. It knows its beauty and displays it. In other words, the creative power when present does not think, "How much will I get for what I give?"

Human beings in most cases, they are ready to receive, but when it comes to giving back they forget – but the Law never forgets. That is the beauty and wonder of it, and when we are open to it we get all its beauty. Therefore, such individuals who create get back from the Law all they created and even more, for since the Law is creative it must also give more back to the individual each time that it expresses itself. This is our second birthright, which we must try to express after we discover and claim it. That is why when we ask, "What shall we do?" of others, it is because of mental laziness. We want to consider people a couch, and often instead of being grateful at having a couch, people blame the couch for being hard. My advice to such is to get off the couch or else don't grumble if the couch is hard or unpleasant.

When we have won our freedom and discover that we can be self-reliant we have gained half of life's battle, but there are two more things to consider – self-determination and happiness.

Each human being has to learn to determine for themselves – it is a part of self-reliance, but it is a step further. The first step is to be self-reliant. Most people have no idea of self-determination. They do not know what they want nor what they don't want, yet there is the urge. But, if we don't know how to determine our course, then it will not produce constructive results, and for this we require discrimination.

You find self-determination everywhere, even among plants. I have seen a seed which grew on a rock become a tree six feet high and when it could not grow more, it didn't want to die, it was determined to live for that was its instinct and self-determination, so what did it do? It began to send its roots outside the rock and finally it reached the soil and the whole of that rock had roots all over it and the tree lived. When we see a tree like that, it is a marvel.

I have known human beings like that. There was one I remember in particular. He was born to die a cripple, yet that man, handicapped in every way by his surroundings for he was of a family, who threw their birds out of the nest before they grew feathers, was intelligent and he was successful and lovable. He was a great living lesson of what a human being can do who has self-determination.

Consider Helen Keller, who overcame every physical challenge, which a human being could expect to encounter and became an example to all.

If one can do this; then all can do it, for every human being is born with the same power latent in them. You may not understand that statement, but Life depends on the totality of its individual manifestations. If one individual among the totality remains a failure, Life is not yet a success; it has still to work out its problems because of that, Life will leave no stone unturned until the last failure becomes a success. That is why you were given the story of the Good Shepherd who leaves his flock to go after the lost sheep, for he must bring it back, and if one of the sheep is missing, he is not a good shepherd. This is the point of the Absolute.

Now, in the approach to our individual lives, it will not work in that way. We have to consider the life of that individual must be sacrificed to the benefit of all.

When humanity will understand this fact, there will be no hesitation on the part of the one called on to give up his life for the life of the many, though he may say – "I have just as much right to live." Now, therefore, why not step aside, so to speak, for the benefit of others? That story of the Good Shepherd is only typical of the operation of the Absolute and not of us human beings, not even of Jesus. Life itself will take good care that whenever an individual puts forth a sincere effort to achieve success it will be on its side because the success of the individual is the success of Life itself. Until the time comes when every destructive vibration, whether in the physical or the mental (as in thoughts,) is entirely eliminated, Life will not consider itself a success.

When this work will be accomplished, Life will progress as it is meant to progress through successive painless unfoldment, on and on and on. Because of our ignorance of these things, human beings have caused more trouble than anything else; as we have mental shutters, so we have bodily gates which we close the moment a progressive force seeks entrance.

The final of our birthrights is Happiness. Happiness should not be something so rare or so difficult of achievement; it is human beings that make it that way. Happiness is a necessity, a fundamental principle of human life, and the most beautiful of all. It is like a golden dome across the temple of our life. Our life should be a temple – a treasure house, of which the outside emblem is that golden dome of Happiness.

Usually, people think that Happiness is somewhere in the future, but this is not so; happiness is always near at hand. Let us recall the words of Goethe, "Why do you want to seek happiness so far away? Happiness is always next to you, close to you. All you need to learn is how to get hold of it now, because Happiness is always at your side." These words are absolutely true. Happiness means joy and harmony. Joy and Harmony are the fundamentals of Life, the foundation and the ultimate, and since this is so, all the things in between partake of the same nature.

Happiness is not a goal; it is a foundation. That is why in looking back into your past you will remember when you were happy and how little things made you so, how everything was much more impressive. Fairy tales were richer because you created a world out of them; you loved the thing you built for you created it; you were happy. What was the Power you felt? It was the creative impulse. The Key to Happiness is the Power to Create. You can't say, "I am going to be happy," or "I intend to be joyful." That is pretense. When you learn to create you will be happy and remember you cannot create anything destructive, it is a misuse of the word. Creative means constructive, if you produce destruction, you do not create, you bring forth destruction.

Everyone of us can create, if not physically, then mentally or emotionally. To create means to radiate. That is why it is the worst thing to be repressed. Depression is wrong, it is a form of repression. Why are we now in the midst of a Depression…Because, humanity has forgotten to create. It became repressed and then depressed, and then it started to destroy itself. Remember, therefore, to create, and if each of us will do our best in that direction, we will conquer the Depression and we will have in so doing achieved Happiness.

1933 WINTER COURSE IN THE SCIENCE OF BEING

Third Lesson: Thursday, December 21st, 1933

Given at the Lightbearers' Auditorium, Montreal, Canada

By Baron Eugene Fersen

MATTER

Conditions throughout the whole world at the present time point very clearly to something fundamentally wrong. What is it that is so fundamentally wrong today? Of course, we all realize that perfection has not been known on this planet for millions of years, and therefore, we have grown used to imperfection, especially since these imperfections usually seemed to adjust themselves. Today not only is there no adjustment, but also there is a peculiar contradictory condition in every department of human life. People do not know where to turn, they change their minds continually; one moment they think one way and then change to another way of thinking. Stability has almost vanished from the general life of mankind.

It is very strange when one analyzes conditions, to behold on one hand the amazing material developments. There seems nothing left to consider but material development. Beyond that there is emptiness so strongly felt that the moment people turn away from the material side of life toward something immaterial, they are confronted with that emptiness. Their hearts feel empty and instead of getting some stimulation, some support from the higher realms, they get nothing but a cold wintry blast causing them to return to the material world with much greater eagerness again to find that they are not satisfied with matter. Like a pendulum they swing from matter across the line to the immaterial, finding satisfaction at no point. People realize they are unable to do without matter and yet they are not content with matter alone. This most complex condition is just as much a puzzle for psychologists as for materialists, but when we approach it from the angle of our teaching it becomes clear.

Now, there we have to do some reasoning because what conditions today show us is not sufficiently convincing, sufficiently proving to us to base our conclusions on that alone. As I said in my last lesson, Life demands to be lived; for this purpose Life seeks by every possible means to persevere in its existence and there are no ends of the planes through which Life can express Itself.

For the time being, we can perceive and understand but three planes, the physical, the mental, and the spiritual. They convey to us the three dimensional conception of length, width, and depth. The concept of length is the first, and the most primitive. Later, when the mind broadens, we have the concept of width and finally when one's mind has deepened it reaches the depth of spiritual perfection.

You cannot have depth without width and you cannot have width without length. Although depth is so important, length is fundamental, for without it the others are not possible of attainment.

It is the same with matter, or rather with what we call matter. Matter is like the first dimension. Now, I didn't say it was the first dimension. It is a foundation without which nothing can be. Next to matter we have the second condition called Mind, and the third dimension called Spirit.

Matter is like an island of ice floating in an ocean of Spirit. The ocean and the ice are the same substance, but ice and water are still different. An iceberg is the product of water combining with cold; the iceberg does not produce the ocean as long as the element of temperature is missing. So, likewise Matter, the opposite of Spirit, floats in Spirit like the iceberg it has its use. The iceberg serves as a refuge for polar bears; it also protects various evidences of life against extreme cold.

Similarly, Matter though a much coarser expression than anything else in nature is still for the time being very essential. For us it is a shelter – a sustaining power. It is a joy too, because Matter properly used gives us joy. Remember, everything which we enjoy is still material, even the most beautiful music is still produced by material means and reaches us through a material medium.

Those we love are, after all, Matter, and through Matter only may we know them, even their inner being is expressed in a material way. How can we be made aware of their emotional responses unless it is through the expression of their eyes, or in words or deeds? Consider what would happen if their material expression should be missing… They would not be in existence for us.

Therefore, no matter in which direction we turn or which dimension we approach, we cannot reach it except through Matter. We cannot approach the soul, or even the Spirit of the Universe except through Matter. You may say that our thoughts are excluded from this statement, but that is not true, for all we can think is the result of the material expression of things we know; the foundation back of it is material.

What do we know about the mental world? It is absolutely a mystery to us. What we know about mental laws and psychology is perceived through material means. In other words, a materialist could do without a spiritualist or a psychologist, but a spiritualist or psychologist could not do without Matter. That is why Kant's philosophy of pure reason is a puzzle. There can be no material reasoning possible without consideration being given to Matter.

The more delicate the material is, the stronger must be the framework. If the material is strong you can have a weak framework, or no frame at all. Take a statue, if carved out of stone or cast from metal, no frame is required, but try to make a wax statue. You will certainly require a framework, for without it the statue of wax will collapse. This shows to what extent we need a framework of Matter in all reasoning.

This is one of the most difficult concepts for human beings to realize and because it is difficult, it produces today an unbelievable confusion of thought. That is why primitive people are more harmonious than our over-civilized people, they accept Matter at its face value, as it is intended to be taken, while we try to explain it away.

You cannot estimate the value of Matter in our daily lives highly enough. All our emotions even of the highest kind based on our relations to the opposite sex would be unrecognizable if Matter were taken away, there would be absolutely nothing left. Emotions do not exclude Matter; they start from the material side. Even when one feels high vibrations inside it requires material channels to express them.

The reason why Matter is so important is that it is an aspect of Life. Matter is Life expressed in a certain form, which enables us to use it as a foundation for further growth. Matter is necessary for Life itself to unfold. For this reason Matter is now imposed, forced on us by Nature herself. This has to be. So far, humanity has overlooked it in their rise upward, but the present material age forces them to see it.

How little people know and know how to get out of Matter all that Matter can give them. Consider a lump of coal; material science today can get all sorts of chemicals, and not only dyes, but perfumes of the most delicate odor. Crude oil, smelling so strongly when distilled, produces perfume. A thing which of itself is muddy looking, can produce the most beautiful colors. Fifty years ago crude oil was crude oil and a lump of coal was just a lump of coal or a mass of oil, but to the scientists it is a vast treasure chest.

I am merely showing you how little Matter was used in days gone by, for naturally if you see a thing in just one aspect, it is not put to much use. But, if you can use it in a multitude of ways you get that much more out of it.

Now consider speed. Do you realize that speed is a material thing? If there were no material instruments to register speed, there would be no speed. It is the same with time – unless Matter is present, time could not exist, for time is the way we register everything in its sequence.

A thing, which happens, is a fact, but how can it happen without material elements? What marks your time or my time or any event in Life? Matter.

As it is in our lives, so it is in the Great Universal Life. Life itself cannot register time without Matter; in other words, without Matter there can be no time. It is the same with Space. Space is not an empty thing. Space is not a vacuum. A vacuum is nothing – Space is something. It is not something encircled by something and called Space. A chair does not stand in Space. A chair determines the space it occupies, therefore, the chair determines the Space.

If we want to be very scientific, we can say the space in the room is determined by the air in it. The old idea of space was a childish one, but today we have a different concept of Space.

There could be no Space unless there was something to determine that Space; it can be a very subtle something – forces, for instance space is determined by forces. I can, therefore, draw the following conclusion: Forces of Nature are material.

Forces are a form of Matter, the subtle form we know of at present; still it is a form of Matter. Thus we have the whole of the Universe transformed into Matter of varying degrees, the lowest easily perceived, the next ascending to such heights that we cannot begin to imagine its subtlety. The ability to perceive the truth of this is one of the greatest achievements of modern science because it will finally discover the cause of all existence. The Causeless Cause, Life Itself in its most powerful and fundamental aspect, in that aspect which includes Matter.

Modern Science will some day discover what we call God, Our

Eternal Father, and Mother also, through material means. That discovery will enable human beings to trace Life upward through the material scale to the origin and there will be no need in those days to ask the question, "Is there a God?" In those days we will know just as we know of Matter today, that there is a Spirit. We will know that it is the highest and most inclusive aspect of that which we call Matter.

Matter is not dead; Matter is all Life, because when you analyze Matter in its secret retreat, we find electrons, neutrons, protons – that is to say, Vibrations – Movement. Matter is Life in a condensed condition and in that concentrated Life, we build our less concentrated Life.

We have to build according to the demands of physical laws, that is why we need Matter and have to understand it and love it as a living substance, as an intelligence, as a Law representing unit, as a loving unit. Once this is understood, its solution will be our greatest triumph.

The ancient Greeks were far superior to others civilizations; for to them a stone was not inanimate, nor a tree a bit of timber. There was a tree Spirit, a Dryad, and a stone Spirit and Spirit resided in everything that was of Life's expression. To them water was not just a chemical equation; it was something living; not only living, but something intelligent. There were nymphs, there was conscious life, friendly life in it, for usually they attributed friendliness to all manifestations of Matter. They recognized the mystery in Matter, and its attraction, and that is why they were so particular in their material works. They understood the true nature of Matter and no one since has grasped this tremendous Truth. The body was sacred to them. The oath of the ancients who were to become physicians was a wonderful one. They put forth the highest principles in the oath of Hippocrates. They loved the body and saw nothing wrong in a naked body. The ancients always contended that in a healthy body, there must be a healthy mind, and yet this simple truth is only now penetrating into our modern civilization.

What happened when religion was introduced into the South Sea Island Natives? The first thing the missionaries did was to point out their nakedness and tell them that if they wanted to find grace they must clothe their bodies. In this manner religion ruined one of the most ancient races on earth, for the South Sea Islanders are the present descendants of the inhabitants of the Continent of Mu. The South Sea Islanders were the pick of mankind, but they were completely ruined by the missionaries who were supposed to help them.

Those who now accuse youth of physical excesses would, if they were pure, really understand the meaning of these excesses. They would realize that they are a misdirection of Life's urge, and that their duty would be to explain it and not just brand those actions as vile and unclean and their bodies impure.

Remember that our body is a sacred entity in which Life - God - dwells. Every door and every ornament in that living temple of ours has a purpose.

There is nothing ornamental in nature; everything has its proper place and the more beautiful they are the more useful they are. If nature did not mean us to have a body, she would not have given us one.

What does our body represent, and what do its parts represent? What are its functions? What is its relation to our mental and emotional side? Modern science is trying to give us the answer. For this purpose we have the Science of Eugenics, of Biology and Pathology.

That is the beauty of knowledge; you discover the best in a thing and you find that further on is a still better understanding awaiting us, for nature gives us all we can assimilate when and as we need it.

That is why the author of Faust who knew, wrote, "Thou art similar to the Spirit you can understand, but not to me." There can only be something in common between you and a Spirit, which you can understand. It is the way nature works.

For this reason things which are clear to some people are incomprehensible to others. We cannot blame such an individual. It may not be lack of desire, it may be lack of development, and unless such a one puts effort into it and works to understand it, he will not be able to do so. It is absolutely necessary that we put our desires into operation; thus we unfold, and what we cannot grasp today will be clear to us tomorrow.

Another thing that religion has fought to remove from circulation is Beauty. Fortunately, in this regard and in spite of all opposition and anathema from the pulpits, it still maintains its position. That element is Woman.

Women as a general rule are in love with Beauty. This is so because women are the embodiment of that part of Life, which is Love. Love without Beauty is not love, and because women are the children of Love,

Beauty is absolutely necessary to them. For this reason they often foolishly exaggerate in their efforts to manifest Beauty. Beauty means so much to them.

To man, Beauty is not so essential until he reaches a higher development. Man's appreciation of Beauty in a woman is not a correct one; man cannot judge rightly for the question of sex enters in.

In beauty contests, women should judge women, yet invariably the judges are men in whom unconsciously sex plays the part of judge and not their ability to appreciate real beauty. Sex, although having a prominent place, is not the whole beauty of the issue. People do not understand Beauty. Beauty means Harmony and the condition of Harmony or Balance, is a fundamental condition of Eternity Itself.

Eternity is based on Beauty and Beauty is Harmony. It is not a curve here and a curve there, or red lips and pink cheeks. Beauty is efficiency; Beauty is the maximum of Power because when you have the maximum of efficiency you find the maximum of Power.

Universal Life builds our body for a certain purpose and that purpose is to make Life more worth living. That is why our body should give us the greatest satisfaction just to live. I spoke to one of our students on these lines and he told me that since he had been on a certain diet he had begun to understand the joy of living.

That is what Life should be for us, enjoyment of every moment – just to be alive should make us feel happy. We don't require all manner of stunts to make us happy. Those who seek physical, mental and emotional stimulants, do so because they are too dead to enjoy being alive.

When one is alive one can be in simple surroundings and enjoy more than those who have everything. The little things of life become really valuable to those who are alive. Consider the young generation, many at twenty are as old as those at fifty or sixty. They are blasé. Why? They are dead. They flit about looking for sensations and call it life. Assuredly, Life is the having of sensations but they must come from within; those who are dead must be whipped from without. Why be whipped by Life when one can be one with Life? That is what the body is for, to unite itself with the air, with the water, with all of Life's vibrations, with others for whom we care.

The aura of the human body mixed with that of another individual, they commune together, they are united. They should enjoy it if their vibrations blend but how different are people's attitudes in that respect. In the youth of today a change is visible, but the old continually look back to the mid-Victorian era. In that respect they keep each other at a distance, in crinolines – they scarcely kiss each other.

But, the body and soul are inseparable, they are not two units. The soul is the vital part of the body, the soul is the center, the directing intelligence of that body. But, when we regard the body as something unworthy, something unintelligent, we fail to see how it can combine with the soul.

The truth is that all cells have intelligence and when one cell fights the general intelligence, it is thrown out, only good cells remain, that is what all bodies do to the derelict in duty.

Our soul is indissoluably connected to the body. The body is a shell, one of many the soul has. Like a snake, which can shed its skin, when the body is outworn it is thrown off and a new, different kind of body is ready for us.

We should try to develop the love of Beauty, which is at the foundation of our being. We should be grateful that it was preserved in womanhood for the saving of mankind through their refusal to listen to the ones in authority who told them, "Away with Beauty." A man who does not love Beauty aside from a pretty girl's face does not live life or get half enough out of it.

All we need to do is look for Beauty and we will find it everywhere. We should not be blind to wrong things, but we should be optimistic. I am called a pessimist for pointing out weakness to you. In particular, do I teach you to see a thing as it is and if it is not beautiful, harmonious, balanced, to do all you can to correct it.

Remember every detail is a little milestone in your life, and while you see these milestones, you need not overlook the house. By so doing you will get more satisfaction from life. Though we must not ignore the wrong side, yet we must put forth all we can on the right side.

One of the many things to make life pleasant is to accept Life – most people when Life offers Itself to them, say "No." You cannot get anything from Life if you close yourself, and when we say "no" we close ourselves, and instead of getting the best, we get the worst. That is why so many take that attitude as a deep one. It is due to the Law of Polarity. When such people meet something new, the Law makes them say "no" even before the thing is stated. Students of the Science of Being know very well that to handle this Law they must rise above it.

When opportunity knocks and the individual says "no" it passes him by, and when the individual reverses and says "yes" it is then too late. That is why people, through not understanding, miss their opportunities.

With the four things I have just explained -

1. Proper diet and care of the body with exercise.

2. The proper understanding of what is wrong with us.

3. To have an open attitude toward Life.

4. And, the love of Beauty.

With these elements you will obtain wonderful results and it will be the best you can do.

The love of Beauty will sound a note of Harmony within you. All the automatic functions of the body will be improved thereby. That is the mental and emotional diet, which should accompany the physical diet. Then only can you say, "I did all I could; I did my best," and you may be sure the result will be good.

1933 Winter course in Science Of Being
Fourth Lesson: Friday, December 22nd, 1933
Given at Lightbearers Auditorium, Montreal
By Eugene Fersen

In my first lesson I spoke to you about the Creative Power of Life itself. I told you that the Power to create is one of the most fundamental we possess. Tonight I will explain how that Creative Power should be used so as to produce the best results in our life.

You are aware that everything has two aspects, an inner and an outer. In the Law of Cause and Effect, cause is the inner and effect is the outer. These two must be harmonized and unless they are, we do not achieve perfection. Harmony is impossible unless the inside and the outside are balanced.

If the outside is overdeveloped, the inside becomes an empty shell and if the inside is overdeveloped it causes jerks and explosions in the outside. Naturally under these conditions there can be no outside harmony, consequently the inside harmony is also then jeopardized.

The first thing to consider is how we can develop ourselves in the best way and how we can adjust the outside in the best way to support our inner selves. The process of self-adjustment is important. If we don't start from the A, B, C's in building our character, we cannot succeed. The human character is the cause of all we do in life and it all depends upon how well or how badly that cause operated. There is continual reaction and inter-relation between the outside world and ourselves. The outside affects us and we in turn affect the outside world or the affects we create affect the outer world and thus it affects us.

If we are undeveloped our surroundings affect us, but if we are well developed we influence our surroundings.

In the beginning a child is almost entirely affected by its surroundings by its mother, for example – In early life a child is not an independent entity at all. Physically it may be, but mentally it is an extension of the Mother hence, it is so important that the parents and especially the Mother be as well balanced as possible. This is the reason it is so important that peace should reign at home even if the child is very small, still its character is affected by its home environments.

The strongest impressions on the mind of a child are those it gets before it is seven. That is why the statement made by some organized religions "Give me the child until it is seven, and you can have it for the rest of its life." To such an extent is the importance of mental influence exercised on the child in its early years recognized by those organized authorities.

We read so much about how parents should bring up children. There are various methods supposed to develop children. They are useful but secondary. There is no greater method to develop children than for the Mother and Father to think the right kind of thoughts, for thoughts are such powerful things, that the child is more affected by a thought than by an action. This may seem paradoxical.

A child seems a little lump of flesh which has continually to educate its body by acts. Yet the child is a much more sensitive lump of flesh than when fully grown. It is infinitely more sensitive to mental and emotional vibrations than adults and there is a reason for it. It is the incarnation of a unity not called human being when it first puts on the shell of flesh. Consequently the child which has come into the status of a human being which has come into earthly life (I did not say earth, because all disembodied souls are still on earth,) is nearer than in its adult state to the time when it was vastly more sensitive to vibrations.

Those who are not yet incarnated in the flesh are naturally much more sensitive than we human beings because they are in the realm of Spiritual Vibrations. Our keenest minds and noblest thoughts cannot be compared with the clarity of thought and the refinement of mind and emotions in those beings before they were born.

If you look back into your past life in retrospect, to the time when you were not only a child but an infant, say when you were one year old, you will begin to realize how your vibrational senses have dulled in the interim.

I did not say you could remember at the time you were one year old, but you can look back now and remember that period. No one can look back in the past at a year old, but as you step backward from your present position in time you will discover that the further you go back the more intensely you felt and your ability to feel today cannot compare with earlier years.

I personally remember how much stronger I felt in every direction when I was a child. We grown-ups when moved by strong emotions or passions no matter how strong they are, cannot compare them in strength with those we had as a child. For this reason parents should be as careful in handling a child as they would be in handling the wing of a butterfly, for if you even caress it too strongly, that beautiful sheen, the delicate scales from which it is made is injured by your touch.

We cannot be responsible for what our parents or our surroundings did to us when we were children that was beyond our control. If a child loses in its fight for self-expression it has a tremendous effect on its later life. It becomes a complex an inhibition and most people carry inhibitions all their lives.

Take an individual in its fullness, in that human unit, we are a triune being, body, mind and soul, yet those three parts are so interwoven that it is hard to say where one ends and the other begins.

We are interwoven in the following way – Most people think of themselves as having three strata – the central or inner, which is the spirit, around which is a coarser one, the mind and beyond that a still coarser one, the body.

But the above is not true at all. Furthermore, if one did not understand the Law, it would be hard to believe the real facts. Our mind is so interwoven in us that we have it even in our feet, our hands. There is no part of the body where soul and mind is not equally present.

You may ask, but is not the mind in the brain? No, the brain is merely a switchboard for certain mental processes. It may seem stronger because the qualities are more concentrated. Nevertheless, the whole of our body has mind and soul interwoven in it.

It is like this: Consider water, alcohol and oil when mixed, they seem like one liquid for you cannot separate the water from the alcohol or the alcohol from the oil. Their union produces a mass of an entirely different aspects or color from any of its individual components. Yet if you look at it through a microscope you will find each one separate but you will find in combination, here - one of water, here – one of alcohol and here – one of oil and naturally as they are so very small, when you look at the emulsion you do not see the individual molecules. They seem to be blended or merged into one mass, yet they are not. Consider muddy water. It seems dirty, yet filter it and see how clear it becomes. Why is this? Because mud does not become one with water, therefore, the moment you pass muddy water through a filter you get the separation.

If we could pass our triune being through some filter we would get matter on one side, mind on another, and soul on a third, but it cannot be done because the being which is non-human would go to pieces.

That such an entity must have a body. The aggregate activities of those beings must be outlined. Everything even light, every vibration is outlined. Everything which is material must be outlined because that is one of the qualities of matter.

Coming back to human beings - When you realize that you are that peculiar mixture of matter, mind, and soul, obviously you will have a much greater respect for your bodily aspect than you ever had before. You will realize much more the importance of harmonious acts, for according to the harmony in those acts will be based the harmony of your body. Harmony can actually change a disharmonious body into a harmonious one. In the education of children, the most important thing is to start to build your own character and you will see how the child builds its own character into its body, patterned on yours.

When the child reaches the age of puberty, the influences of the parents wanes and its own character takes form. It is only that it becomes fit for procreation.

No matter how highly we consider a child, it is still incomplete until it reaches puberty because as I said in another lesson, the creative power is essential for everyone and everything. It is fundamental for us human beings. Therefore, until that Power is capable of being expressed in full, the human being cannot be called complete. The period of puberty is one of which we must be very careful, for the making or unmaking of an individual can take place at that time.

You may have observed that when anyone passes through that period, suddenly out of a comparatively formless mass of flesh there appears the final structure. Often in less than a year a girl or boy can undergo a greater change than during the rest of their lives.

It is like carving from matter of an indefinite form something very precise. Why is it that sometimes that carving is done very strongly and produces a very outstanding personality, some on the contrary remain very ordinary in appearance? One reason for this difference is that during the period of puberty the youngster was able under certain stimulus, which is first of all transmitted from the glands, to mold his body in accordance with the character forming within.

There are many glands known by science today but which are still a mystery when one has to explain their working. They are in the final analysis stimulated by the soul, the Power behind the Earthly Throne, to produce amazing changes in the human body. We call those changes Characteristics and they are both inherited and acquired. The parents therefore, for the sake of the children, if for no other reason, should live a harmonious life particularly prior to the age of puberty of their children. They should give them the opportunity to make this change under the best possible conditions.

The youngsters should be taught the importance of sex life. The fear which people have in supplying this information to the young is one of the greatest curses to growing humanity. The ancient myth that the eating of the fruit from the Tree of Knowledge was a sin could only have been found in a perverted religion. In this criticism, I am not referring to the teachings of those on whom such religions were founded. I mean that which we later on grafted onto the original, beautiful and very practical teachings brought to humanity by World Teachers from age to age. Their teaching was correct but the grafting was entirely wrong. The story of the apple was not originated by Moses but taken from Babylonian Mythology; also the Ten Commandments cut in stone so attributed to God and to Moses or as some think, first to Moses and then to God, are not at all the work of Moses. They were copied verbatim from Babylon. There are records that Hammurabi, thousands of years before Sinai had them in Babylon on almost every street corner.

From this source also comes the Tree of Knowledge myth, only it was not as stated in the Bible. They were not punished for eating the fruit of the Tree of Knowledge.

Knowledge is the most precious thing there is and the curse lies not in eating but in not eating and yet religions call it original sin. This is in relation to the fact that unless we know certain things about sex and its various aspects and the way it expresses itself, we usually make terrible mistakes. That is why the young people of this generation who have acquired a measure of their knowledge with no thanks to their uninformed parents and with all their excesses, are more moral and less perverted than the older generation.

To the old generation, sex is something obnoxious, yet they are very interested. The young generation freely discusses it and greatly benefit thereby; not all, of course, for there are still old fashioned young people whose attitude is colored by their surroundings and education. Today youngsters are cleaner than those of other ages. Yet from the pulpit we find continual criticism nowadays – they never cease to bemoan the immorality of this age.

Remember, it is very important to realize that as long as a thing arouses within you a sense of indecency it is because you have within you a thing which vibrates to that tune. There is something guilty within the deep recesses of your being.

So, when you hear a preacher speak against the moral life of others you can rest assured that there is something unclean in him/her. The very thing they condemn they have within them, yet hate to acknowledge it and so exteriorize it in diatribes.

The moment we do not have that sense inside us we are no more in judgment, we do not get angry or indignant over it. We take it calmly and make the proper step to remove it.

I am giving you a very important point in self-analysis applicable to any situation. The most important thing is to build our character. It is incomplete and consequently our mind must adapt it accurately to the mandate of our Soul and in that process of character building we must know what are our shortcomings. Otherwise we will believe ourselves very much better equipped than we are because remember, the strength of the chain is always in its weakest link. We don't need to discover our strong points but our week spots. The best way to discover our weak spots is to see how we react to certain situations. There again, there is a very great difference between facing a certain condition outwardly calm but inwardly boiling and the reverse when we seem to explode outwardly and yet remain calm inside. Those who act according to the latter method do so because they are full of vitality, they boil over in any direction but inside they are calm. Then there are, as I said those who are outwardly calm and inside are a seething volcano. Of the two, the best to be calm inside, but neither is a perfect as being calm both inside and outside. Thus our outside is in tune with our inside and vice versa. Then we get the best results. When there is a conflict between the outside and the inside, there is no harmony, there is loss of power. For this reason human beings should not live alone. They should seek opportunity to contact the outside world for they need to balance the inside reactions with outside influence.

To be a recluse is not right. A human being can only achieve proper development amidst his fellow beings, even if we do not like their company, still they will do some good to us by bringing out our shortcomings.

In this manner we are able to see ourselves in a light we may not like but we should be grateful to those who bring the dark parts of our nature into the light where we can take steps to eradicate them. We don't need to worry about the good in us but we must take care of the spots that tarnish the brightness of our character, and when this is done the next step is to clean them.

The above is entirely opposite to the attitude of mental science and metaphysics which tells us to keep an aloof attitude toward the whole of life. If we keep aloof there is penalty. Life keeps aloof from us as an immediate and direct result of our attitude and if Life keeps aloof from us, there is no greater loss. Likewise that aloofness which says – "I don't want to do anything about this, is that wrong if it is no concern of mine?" is detrimental.

There are also racial antagonisms between the races; these utter dislikes of anyone who is not of the same race as another is a terrible and destructive thing. It actually takes away ones inborn nobility of character. One human being who looks on another with contempt because of a difference in color is thereby demonstrating themselves to be a contemptible being.

I am throwing a big stone against hundreds of millions of people when I say that there is no race that is inferior to the Great Principle. I want you to realize the truth of this is based on the fact that no one can feel contempt unless they have it in them. The more you hate the more hateful you are yourself; the more contemptuous you feel, the more contemptible you are. If you are indignant about something, that something is in you. These are truths which the world is not yet ready to acknowledge.

Most people try to build character until they reach the age of 25 or so and after that, especially if successful materially they abandon the attempt to continue building their character. You all have seen successful business people. What sights they are. They are usually physically, mentally and spiritually suffering. It is hardly believable that they were once young and full of enthusiasm or that they smiled at Life and Life smiled at them. When you find a person who sees materially enough as never being enough you have see a piggish element has developed there in them. In a pig it is all right to look like a pig but for a human being to deteriorate like that is not the right use of their Power.

Such people consider that because they have Power they don't need to bother about character. They fail to realize that the more powerful we become the more the Law demands that our character grow. Human beings may not think so – they may forgive almost everything in a man with Power. Often petty thieves are put in jail but the big ones escape and are put on a pedestal as an outstanding citizen.

A really outstanding thing has its own natural pedestal and it does not require to be put on one, it is already there. In many instances the so-called successful individual himself climbs on a pedestal and as the public will tolerate anything they accept his own valuation. That is not real recognition of a true sense of value.

When an individual reaches so-called success in life, he pays for that with his higher self. That is an abnormal condition and contradictory. It is the very opposite of all those Laws of Nature and of the very principle of Life itself.

Life demands that even if we can't grow any other way, we should grow in character. When we die we leave behind all our wealth, our bodies; everything but our character which is not affected by the flesh of our body.

That character of ours, when our being leaves its earthly shell, is there to help us take an advance step in that life which it is to live on the other side. That is why those who brought wonderful messages to mankind to build character, emphasized that humanity should care more for the Spiritual values than for the material.

When we take proper care of that body into which our youthful forces build a character up to the age of 25, then it is that we should consider taking up that character and build it finer, broader and deeper in every direction. This should remain our foremost aim on Earth.

There is no excuse that we are too old. What is age? The soul is not old, it is only our consciousness that seems old, even the cells can live and grow indefinitely. It is the violation of those various Laws that bring old age on our body. Therefore, no human being is excused from making their character into the best they can and to continue to improve it during their lifetime. For the day will come for us to answer to our own selves. We may not answer as a human being but some day we shall have to answer. There is a great deal of advantage in carrying out this advice.

Consider the artist who draws a picture, he/she will continually seek to improve on it, a musician, a composer, a sculptor, a scientist, - all never satisfied with their work, they know that there is so much more to do to improve it.

The building of our character and the using of those creative powers within us is the most interesting work we can do, not as poor prisoners but as free beings. None of us are really free, we made ourselves prisoners in this human body or ours. With most human beings their body is not a temple – it is just a nasty prison.

We should never be satisfied to be in that prison but should try to build the best into our character and thus liberate ourselves from that prison and make ourselves the master of the house. That is all we need and that is one of the most important aims for every human being and when this is achieved, we are ready to create, so to speak, outside and there we have the help of the outside to make the inside finer and better.

Every expansion of the inner influences the outer and that in turn reacts again on the inner and thus we make our lives entirely different from other people and obtain complete peace in the midst of the trouble around us. Thus we may have better health and affluence while around us is poverty and sickness. Do not expect a sudden change to occur to your character but sooner or later the work must be done, for real character is part of Universal Harmony. Some may say "I don't care to take the trouble," but it is not true, for everyone cares to be happy and nobody can enter that state without developing their character. It may take us life after life, incarnation after incarnation, so why not start now?

There is another point I want to impress on you. Life is like a race and the building of character is like a race also. We may not be strong enough not to lose but we should not worry – but pick ourselves up and continue the race.

So many fall and sit or lie while they groan and yet do nothing; we must remember but not be affected by the fall. The falls should be burnt into our mind, yet it must stimulate us to continue. No matter how many times you fall, still continue the race and some day you will reach the goal.

Sequel to Lesson 4 –Dec 22nd 1933:

In reply to a statement on remembering when one is very young, Svetozar said: "I explained to you that we could not remember at the time when we were very young but we can remember that period now that we are grown up".

Miss Tyler asked him if he remembered previous incarnations. He replied: "It is impossible to state this positively, for one can only really remember what can be proved a fact to our own satisfaction. The human mind is liable to magnify their own thoughts and believe them facts, but unless they can be proved, that cannot be considered as evidence of remembering past lives. I have met at least four people in my life that imagined they were Cleopatra – one of them happened to be a man." In reply to Mr. Mears, he said: "I did not say that one could not be convinced that they had lived before as a certain personality but unless they can prove it, there is no use discussing it".

1933 WINTER COURSE IN THE SCIENCE OF BEING

Fifth Lesson: December 26, 1933

Given at the Lightbearers' Auditorium in Montreal, Canada

By the Baron Eugene Fersen

We all know that our power to think proves that we are alive. The mere fact that we can say, "I think, therefore, I am," is evidence of one of the most important qualities we possess. If it were not for Intelligence, Life would not be worth living for it is only that quality that makes Life what we perceive it to be.

The more that quality of the mind develops the more Life increases in interest and beauty. The fundamental quality of Life is to create, but it creates only Life, what we may term formless material. It is due to the Power of the Mind that it is put into the proper form, color and arrangement.

That formless unit which Life creates is chaos, but with Mind in operation it has a chance to become harmonious. A chaotic condition is only made into an orderly one because Mind uses its Power to organize. Thus, we have that extraordinary Universe around us, working to such perfection due entirely to the operation of Mind.

The human mind unfortunately does not work according to that ideal pattern. What I explained is something ideal, that Intelligence in solution which permeates, guides and governs the whole Universe. Outside of us Law and Order prevail and intelligence rules supreme. Inside of us is entirely different as our Intellect is not a ruler, our Intelligence is a prisoner, and because our Intelligence has been deviated from its seat of Power where it was intended to rule, it is dwelling in what we actually may call a prison.

What can a prisoner do? In most cases, first in prison, he has no desire to do anything. His thinking cannot be along constructive lines. There seemingly is no hope for a prisoner; and the days seem to be as long as years, and the years appear to be an eternity.

This is exactly what our human mind feels today – it feels in prison. It is distressed. It has little hope. It does not think constructively. There would be no evil, trouble or wrong around us if there were not so much wrong inside of us.

Our mind supplies all the wrong we find on this earth, even beyond, for as the earth's atmosphere extends far beyond the earth, so our mental atmosphere extends into the beyond, the unknown part of the existence which is beyond the gates of earthly life. Even there we will find the same disharmonious ways of thinking so prevalent here on earth.

Because Mind is imprisoned, it does not think constructively, and because of that the majority of people have no interest in Life. Like prisoners, they perform their daily tasks as in a prison. They eat, they sleep, they even go to Church or play games, but no matter what they do they cannot dope themselves. They can never forget that they wear a prisoner's garb, striped black and white.

Do you know that the similarity between a prisoner and ourselves consists in the stripes we both wear? In these stripes you see opposing colors, though they are complimentary in a way, yet in another they represent the operation of the Law of Polarity. The Law of Polarity is like the garb of a prisoner, it is a law which as long as we are subject to it, no matter where we go or what we do, will always make us appears as prisoners. It points out to somebody else, "that is a prisoner."

The Law of Polarity in us causes us to realize the extent to which we are in chains. This is a point very few people understand; even some of the most advanced thinkers do not grasp it properly. They have an inkling, but it appears so hopeless to them that they prefer to leave it alone, and if they do discuss it what they have to say is so hopeless that it would have been better left unsaid.

We Lightbearers who know the Science of Being should have the courage to approach the subject in a direct manner. There is no use to beat around the bush. People have tried it for countless generations without results.

People today are in a very advanced age in the life of mankind. That alone demands productiveness, and if a thing is not productive it is thrown overboard from the ship of Life. It is useless – it is much more dangerous to carry a useless burden.

We may carry a burden, food for instance, but that is useful to us. But, if we carry a burden of food with us when we can get better food in an instant, it is not productive thinking. Today humanity realizes that such ways should be discarded completely. There is no limit to the books today that deal with all sorts of metaphysical questions, but when you read them you merely mentally exercise your mind. It is a species of gymnastics, because they are not productive. People think them wonderful, but such people are not really intelligent.

Real intelligence is only present when used productively, and the moment a person uses their Intelligence unproductively that person is lacking in Intelligence. It is merely a form of conceit for such a person to consider it otherwise.

The above happens to so many so-called intelligent people. They do not know how to be Intelligent, and in the general economy of Life such people will be dealt with as they deserve.

There are no useless units in Life. They are either constructive or destructive – nothing is neutral. In nature one is hot or cold, constructive or destructive, but one cannot be the one and the other. That is a condition, which we are unable to conceive, and a thing we cannot conceive is of no use to us.

We can only approach anything by asking – "How much will it help me?" or "How much will it interfere with me?" Therefore, people such as I have described are worse than useless – they are destructive, and in nature when anything, whether it be a law or anything else, becomes useless, it is thrown overboard. This is one of the 'peculiar' modern ways of thinking, but instead of taking away the glamour, poetry or romance, even if they seem to do so, such a way of thinking gives more than it takes away. In place of mere illusion we get the romance of reality, the poetry of truth.

A fact can be of more value to you and more interesting than just a dream. Instead of romance, something invented by our mind; we are able to replace it by Truth. In reality, Truth is much more romantic than any fiction. Truth is not destructive, and anything, which is absolutely true, must be constructive. Truth really appears to anyone, who can face it directly, in the most beautiful colors; it is a regular rainbow of Life, and like the rainbow it connects earth with heaven. It connects the domain of the Invisible with the realm of the Visible.

When we have Truth we don't need Romance, and in every line of thinking, when we have that which is actual, we do not need any illusion. Far better one sparrow in our hand than ten in the bush; better one dollar in our pocket than to think that someone will promise you ten and not give it.

In other words, only facts count for only facts can be produced. You may ask, does our way of thinking make us creative? The mere fact that we are already thinking productively, meaning constructively, makes us create that reality. It may be very intangible, yet it is real.

The next step is not to translate that into the physical plane but to plant that mental seed which we conceived into the material life around us. It is a very easy process and a normal one for normal people, particularly to people who have not overbalanced their mental qualities. These physical and mental planes should be correlated; even if they do not know the mental laws, such people do it unconsciously.

The planting of a mental concept into physical ground is done as follows: You conceive an idea and you go about realizing it. You have not the right to conceive anything mentally which you do not put into material expression, because even mental concepts must be born as a physical child on the plane of matter; unless we do so we do not fulfill our duties as creators.

The Power of Procreation, which means to produce physically, is not as important as the Power of the Mind to Create, but the Power to Create must be manifested. That is why so often we see people with plenty of ideas, and yet they seem to achieve very little in their lives, because they do not give birth to their mental children. The moment we conceive a mental child, and our discrimination tells us it is worthwhile, we should do all we can to manifest it.

We must be careful of our mental ideas, for they stick in our subconscious and become deeply engraved there, whereas on the physical plane they are easier to alter. For instance, one may write a wrongly constructed sentence and erase it just as easily, leaving very little trace, but you cannot do that on the mental plane. All that is done when we think we erase a mental concept is to cover it up. It is still there until the opportunity arises for it to come to the surface.

Furthermore, those who are prolific of ideas on the mental plane but scarce of results on the physical are not only useless, but also dangerous to their fellows.

In this Universe in which we live, the Power of Energy is limitless. None of it should be wasted, and when we incur that waste, particularly mental waste, we violate a principle. To waste physical things is wrong, but it is of lesser account compared to wasting mentality.

Although the Power of the Universe is limitless, still if drawn on more by one human being than by another, then the latter has less than he should have. It may seem unreasonable that this can be possible when we are dealing with an unlimited Infinite Power, but it is like this:

Take a vacuum cleaner and place it over a lake. When the machine is started the water in the lake will rise up, drawn by the suction of the air in the cleaner. Next to the point where the water rises, will be found a depression, and yet there is water in abundance all around, and when the machine sucking the water is stopped, the surface of the water becomes level again. It is an example of the operation of the Law of Rhythm.

If some individual takes plenty of mental energy to create mental thoughts, to a certain extent, like the vacuum cleaner, he takes away a corresponding amount of Power from someone else, and, as it was not used it was wasted. No one is benefited and in fact, all are harmed. Better not to attempt too many things, but to dedicate your efforts with intention and direction to making one idea a reality.

Mental gymnastics are a poor satisfaction, for we are in spite of all our mental Powers, still living on the Physical and not the Mental Plane. Until the Physical Plane is molded and polished like a mirror by our effort into perfection, we will be unable to step into the next plane.

As I explained to you before, the so-called three planes of our present existence are really one Plane. It is really Spirit under these aspects, or Matter, under three aspects, depending on whether you approach the physical from below or from above.

From below you have the material, then mental and Spiritual, but these are still two additional planes of matter. If you approach it from the top, you have the mental, which is also an aspect of that same Spiritual Power. It is like climbing a mountain; think what results you can achieve if you start at the bottom of the mountain and climb step by step to the top. Compare the intimate knowledge of the Mountain of Life, thus acquired, to what you would obtain if you leapt at once to the top and surveyed the valley below. You no longer see the bottom clearly, and what use is it to regard the bottom in a fog, since your objective in climbing to the top is to survey the country at the bottom.

You can by mental gymnastics leap to the top of that mountain – it is very interesting – but it is not likely to produce the best results. The important thing is to explore the bottom, step by step ascending. Thus, you learn in the best possible way to overcome deep crevasses. You can only surmount a crevasse by climbing it, not by gazing at it from the top after leaping over it. This should show you clearly that the practice of teachings based on mental considerations alone tries to leap to the top ignoring and denying matter.

Such systems of thought succeed because they appeal to human vanity. Human beings are so vain that while they are on the bottom they delude themselves into thinking that they are at the top. They are still worms crawling on this planet, and it is only when they crawl up the Mountain of Life, by actually making the effort, and every moment adjusting themselves to new conditions and the contour of the land, that they are able to advance.

But, the above viewpoint is what some of the most advanced thinkers refuse to accept. That is why they cannot achieve the immense advancements of Edison, Ford, or Marconi. These, indeed, are great geniuses, and show the heights to which mankind can achieve in various directions.

Consider the beauty of some mental concepts, but as long as they are not put into practical circulation, of what use are they. To dream and dream of beautiful things is of no value. This is what happens when a part of humanity becomes affiliated with different religions. They become dreamers and not doers. They dream and dream themselves through, leaving what trace in Life? Dust – that is all they left – dust. Life is not dust. Life is a glorious pulsating, moving, thinking, loving unit. It is only those who are ordinary wide awake human beings who understand the requirements of Life, and who, although they had visions of heights, did not despise that which is close at hand. They knew that they could make beautiful and useful things out of clay, such as porcelain and china, or turn brick into building, and who knew that in the earth they could discover gold, oil, etc.

In other words, the conquest of time and space has created those great mental limitations, which our own human mind has imposed on us.

Those who could take brass and other metals and shape them into beautiful forms have created a wonderful part of our present civilization, and helped make Life so much better to live despite the many difficulties yet remaining. As this continual advance and constant improvement proceeds, Life will be even more worthwhile, so let us, in pondering on the relative values offered by various types of human beings, give the credit to the doers rather than to the dreamers who do nothing.

Many of those who were considered great in days gone by have today lost their reputation because they were not producers, and only that which is produced has the right to endure. I believe all of you who listen to me realize that I am not one who considers it necessary to deprecate that which I do not understand.

I do not throw a stone at mental capacity because I lack the mental capacity to understand, but having reached a certain age, after experiences which have made me many times older mentally than corresponds to my actual years, I came to the conclusion that we have to give a prominent place to matter. On it, we have to found everything, and through which we have to work out the problems of our life. The mistakes, which I have made in my life, were because I let my mental side unbalance my other sides.

For instance, if I had paid more attention to the material side, in its respect to my own material surroundings, the teachings of the Science of Being would have been a fact accepted by the whole of humanity. I would then have had the material means to put into effect my productive thinking.

In days gone by, people were able to get along without money. Yes, because in those days the manifestation of the higher laws and forces on this material plane were entirely different from what they are today. This is the beauty of Life, it is never the same two moments, it is always changing like everything in Nature always changes, yet it is immutable as a fundamental. It is a unit, which is immutable in that respect, but which always is, always has been, and forever will be unceasingly. The same in nature fundamentally, but continually changing, varying all the time.

That is why to be set in our ways, crystallized, is utterly wrong, because we oppose the very principle in us which continually demands change. The best we can say is, "That is as far as I will go today." You can only measure the thing you have in front of you, but you cannot measure a thing of which you have no conception.

You cannot measure the skies, yet they are in front of you, you are not measuring them in the future, for it is with light that it reaches you now. What is here is the only thing that counts; what is there is beyond human comprehension. That is why Life is not practicable to people who don't understand this.

Today we must measure the complete thing we do. There are no chapters tomorrow. Tomorrow is a new chapter. Wherefore say, I will finish a thing tomorrow? This does not mean that we should not plan for tomorrow. You never hear me say that, but your plans should not be rigid, impossible to alter. Your plans must be elastic; we must be flexible. That is why those who are rigid cannot do productive thinking, they cannot expand when necessary or contract when required, or overflow when expedient, or retract when advisable.

At times we must draw into a hole – we cannot always be in a superstructure. Sometimes we are like the outside of a tree, sometimes we are like its roots, underground, sometimes we are solid like a rock, and sometimes as light as a feather. Unless we are that way we would not be like a microscope as well as a telescope. We have endless facets to reflect life, and this is what people would do if they were not immovable.

People imagine that they are alive because they laugh a little, move a little, eat a little, sleep a little – yet we could live and make our lives so wonderful.

All this is according to the Law of Cause and Effect. When we plant a good seed we will reap a good result. Why not do so? Some go through Life sowing constructive seeds; they make mistakes, yet if they are intelligent they will not make so many and learn from those that do transpire.

Above all, do not be afraid to express, for fear of making mistakes. The greatest mistake human beings can makes is to fear to make mistakes. Without them where is the learning, the evolving?

That brings us back to what I have so often advised you. Let us be ourselves. It is not easy in this world today.

Think always in such a way as to act constructively in every direction. It will not demand a great amount of energy, for there is something within us that enables us to guide our will like a compass guides a ship, almost automatically.

We have within us all that Mother Nature gave us. Mother Nature is a real Mother. She has not thrown us into Life to sink, but to float. She gave us all we need, and that is what we call that Inner Guidance, Intuition, whereby one feels one must do a thing, follow that hunch. Learn to know when it is a right one.

So often we want to say something to somebody, the thing is on our tongue, and yet we don't say it. Later we discover that if we had said it or done it, we would have been successful.

We should not let these things pass by for they are big things after all and are a part of our productive thinking.

Before I close I wish to point out something that will help you to fit yourself to the changing conditions which will be more and more evident as time passes. Events and things will move quicker and quicker until the end of the cycle is reached. Then will come peace and quiet, but it will not be in laziness or inaction. When a new cycle will become a reality, then all that peace and quiet will become visible, but at first it will be hardly perceptible, and in that time people can seek rest but it must be rest in proper activity. They will be able to breathe and not hurry, and they will say – "Here we have a breathing space," but this will be due course giving place to further speed, until it exceeds the speed of the previous cycle. When the last cycle ends, then all that which the last cycle has achieved becomes the foundation of the new cycle, which is really the continuation of the old.

The reason why Life seems to become pleasanter than at the end of the previous cycle is because the majority of people could not stand the continual sequence of events unfolding. That is what we see today. How can anyone follow what occurs at this time?

Change occurs at different rates, according to where we are on our path.

By what we see around us today we can judge what will happen tomorrow. Today we are coming to the end of this present cycle. When it will actually end, no one can tell, for it depends on the way people are thinking, even on the sun spots, because in that world where we live everything forms a connecting link. We are intimately connected with the Sun. The Earth is the child of the Sun. So what happens on the Sun has a tremendous influence on the atmospheric conditions on Earth. Some scientists even claim it affects our way of thinking, and why not? Are not our bodies elements of the same as those of the Sun, and when a change in them takes place it should reflect their counterpart in our body.

Most scientists fail to see this because there is hardly one of them whose knowledge is not specialized. They cannot therefore take in things as a whole. No one can be compared to Aristotle in breadth of vision.

No one since Aristotle has achieved his universality of knowledge. There have been some like Leonardo da Vinci whose knowledge was phenomenal, but even his equal is not to be found today. The great scientists of today are specialists in their particular field, but they are by no means broadly equipped with knowledge of other branches. This accounts for the lack of collaboration and their tendency to fight among themselves. Their extremely pointed attitude causes their minds to become incapable of grasping the depth of thinking in all directions, and although they may be wonderful in one direction, if they cannot go further they are still blind.

All this is a process of evolution. We have been specializing, and when this process approaches its limit, then as the specialists have filled themselves completely as individuals, they must overflow into their fellow beings, thus bringing up the general level of knowledge around them. When this process is completed, the specialist is submerged, they no longer stand out like rocks in the ocean, and their knowledge becomes united into one common collective.

This is what will happen in the comparatively near future, then we will be collectively as great as Aristotle. He was not the ultimate, for in the centuries since his time humanity has progressed and become much more diversified.

There was once a half-mythical being called Hermes Trismegistus, a Pharoah of Egypt, the Messenger thrice blessed. That is, blessed on the physical, mental and spiritual planes. He was as universally minded as any human being could be, yet today should be greater than yesterday, so even Trismegistus should be excelled by one or more beings today. Aristotle was all that was needed then, but today knowledge is spread all over the earth, so we need many such beings that are able to foster and possess in themselves a universality of knowledge.

When this condition happens once more, as it will inevitably, the cycle will again produce specialization, and those specialists in turn will raise the general level. That is the spiral course of evolution. We are a part of that evolutionary process. Therefore, in order to further these results; do not hold to anything old. Remember, if you follow a rigid line, you will not be able to follow the continual changes now intensifying, which demand flexibility.

The only thing you should do is to remain true to yourself. It is like this: Water, no matter the vessel it is in, whether square, round or any other shape, is always water. Be like a liquid. Remember…when you are required to do so, you can freeze any liquid solid, you can also convert it to vapor.

You can, if necessary, make yourself solid, and you can make yourself into a vapor, but in all this process, remember you are still to be yourself. So be adaptable, if not to that extent on the physical, at least mentally as regards character. There is a continual change going on within us. For example, I heard recently of someone who had read a certain book a year ago. He found nothing in it, but now, a year later, he read it again and discovered that he was intensely interested in it. Why? He had changed in that span of time. This is not an undesirable condition, it is an absolute necessity.

To be moody, temperamental and changeable is an entirely different thing. To be moody is not to know what you want or what you should do. To hesitate, to be moody, is to be in a muddy mental condition, and that is highly undesirable.

To be temperamental is not to know what one wants. It is the same as moodiness, and is equally undesirable. It is a surface effect, not a real change, which is from within.

The best we can do to adapt ourselves to our surroundings is to face life as it is and try to get the best adjustment, and if tomorrow demands of us the opposite course from today, and it seems right to us, we should do it. It is a lesson we must learn. Above all, do not regret the past. The past is gone and has fulfilled its mission. All the old traditions it represents are outlived. We are in a quest for the new. Life is too big a thing to adjust itself to us, we have to go half way, and Life will then meet us at the midpoint.

After finishing the lesson, Svetozar asked: "Did you all feel the mental heaviness during this session?" Several said, "Yes." He continued, "It was because I was trying to awaken you and you did not like it. This produces a natural reaction within you, which is translated into the physical feeling of sleepiness. Remember also, that you are a part of mankind, as drops of water in the ocean are a part of the ocean, and that you react to the general condition as a whole. If you push a particle of water in an ocean, the reaction will be perceived at the other end of the ocean though thousands of miles away, for nothing is ever lost."

SPIRITUAL LESSON – DECEMBER 29, 1933

Lecture by the Baron Eugene Fersen

Described by Miss M. Jackson

At this present time we are experiencing a spell of unusually severe cold weather. Now this has significance for us all. This cold wave which is sweeping the world, making every human being shrink within himself to seek for some place where he can find a feeling of warmth, is a manifestation of something which is going to strike us all, not merely in a physical way, but mentally and spiritually. In the future we shall see humanity growing colder and colder towards each other in a mental and spiritual way. There is no way to save ourselves from it. I am sorry to say my friends, we shall all perish from it. We shall feel alone; everywhere will be that cold, mental wall which we shall be unable to pierce. The cold will be terrible. What suffering we shall endure will be worse than physical suffering from cold weather. This will pass, but to prepare ourselves for the long night coming to all mankind, begin now to fan that spark of love within you. Keep it glowing as long as you can, for only by it, will you be able to obtain a sense of warmth during that piercing cold.

You all know how short the days become during the beginning of winter and how long and cold the nights are. Humanity is now facing a winter's night, a long, cold night which will seem never-ending and only by fanning that spark of love, kindling a warm friendship which will last during the cold, will we be able to pull through. The night will pass but not before mankind has suffered and that law, the survival of the fittest, will have operated. Then will come the springtime, and those who have survived the winter will be able to enjoy the warm sunshiny days of spring. There will be the dawn of a new day in which mankind will have risen to higher understanding, enabling him to love his fellowman and journey on, lending a helping hand instead of trying to crush or rise above his fellow being.

THE LEGEND

(Spiritual Lesson)

A beautiful landscape is presented to our mind's eye. In the foreground, admiring the beauty of Mother Nature, are thirteen wondrous beings; they are friends, sons of Light. One among them appears to be their Leader. As they recline, drinking in the beautiful landscape from their position on the mountain top, the one speaks to his friends thus: "How wonderfully perfect everything has been created." And, as he continues to gaze upon the beauteous works of The Creator, the urge to create also awakens within him. So great is this urge that he speaks of it to his friends and they, one and all, approve of his words and beseech him to follow that urge and show them that which he can create for they deem him the greatest among them.

For long he ponders over the question, yet he can find no fault with the work of The Creator – everything is perfect as can be. But, after a period whose duration we cannot estimate in that timeless region, he turns to his twelve friends and with a frown upon his face a dark light in his eyes, he brings forth out of his mind, a creation. He will, he tells them, multiply the beauties of Nature and shows his friends how he and they too can make others like unto themselves – the mountains grow in number, the birds and every living thing is to multiply.

As he speaks to his friends they behold a mirror within which they see themselves. It is the first time they see what superb beings they are. They continue to gaze into this mirror and as they do the mirror seems to grow in length until it encircles them within its walls, and they become prisoners of illusion. They behold themselves in great numbers and all creation appears to grow by leaps and bounds. Beholding this, they acclaim their favored one, greater even than the Creator, greater than Nature Herself. But, as they talk among themselves, the circular walls of the mirror seem beclouded, great chaos arises among the multitudes of people; all their creation changes before their eyes from a thing of beauty to one of ugliness and disgust. Friend kills friend, selfishness reigns, nowhere is there Harmony.

Seeing this reflection in the mirror, the twelve take flight and three run north, three run south, three run east and three run west. The one, once glorified, wonders what he has done to the ones he loves better than his own life. He is so sorry for them that thinking over all he has created in his mind, he perceives with great error. Such is his love for his friends that he seeks a way out of all this chaos and decides to smash the mirror, even knowing that his act will cause misery of his own mind's creation and its effect. With a mighty stroke he breaks the mirror and there is heard a noise like thunder, which shakes the foundations of the world and a flash of light like lightening is seen as the walls crash in and all perish and he too is buried in ruins.

Amid a beautiful scene in peaceful surroundings, we see twelve beings sleeping on the ground with faces turned towards the thirteenth. The first streak of dawn appears and it throws its glow over them. The one who is the leader awakens, he perceives the light rising in all its splendor, throwing its rosy hues over the beauties of the world, the perfect creation of all things by the Infinite. Filled with the wonder and glory of it, he awakens his friends with a gentle, loving touch so that they too may rejoice in being alive and conscious of such perfection, such Harmony. As they open their eyes they one and all look at him with a questioning gaze, and knowing what the question is, with a glance of burning love, he answers, "My friends, it was but a dream."

DO THE DEAD COME BACK TO LIVE AGAIN?
Seattle, Washington – October 2, 1944

Lecture by the Baron Eugene Fersen

Greetings to everybody…This may seem a strange question, one which may mislead quite a few into thinking we intend to discuss the so called Beyond. But, there is something much more important for us to take care of, this life we live here.

The dead who come back, must be reborn. That rebirth is called reincarnation. Reincarnation is very little known in the Western world, yet a billion human beings in the East have believed in it for thousands of years.

It has been asked of what use is that belief to eastern people when they live under such unsatisfactory conditions, while we in the West are so much better off. It seems that way, but actually success in life is not to be measured in monetary terms. We in the United States have developed an entirely false concept of happiness. We think we can buy happiness with money.

It can't be done. Though I believe we in the US are well-natured and well-intentioned people, I think that we are the most unhappy people on Earth. I judge that from over fifty years of observation of this country. I know both the East and the West, and I can tell you that the eastern people who believe in Reincarnation, for all their poverty are much happier than we with all our finery and materialism.

That belief in reincarnation has given them a hope, not in a heaven or hell of the Beyond, but of attaining better in this life. You never see a good tree grow from an inferior seed. If humans are in an unsatisfactory condition in this life, probably that same condition will continue in the Beyond.

Reincarnation is a much more logical concept. Instead of believing that after a poor life here, a wonderful one will suddenly come in the Beyond. And, even that Heaven of harp players sitting on the clouds is not so attractive.

Are those people who believe in reincarnation, so under control of religion that we can't imagine it? Has that caste system been so imposed on people that it over rides even that belief in reincarnation? Yet, even with that limitation of fixed castes, the pariah still has the hope that if he leads a proper life he will be reborn in a better family of pariahs, in a better location, with a better master.

So, even there that belief gives hope to those with little to live for; even in the worst conditions they know that if they do their best they will find better in the next life here. Those people are not foolish, they are mighty intelligent and someday they will throw off that yoke, for they have a leader from Brahmins, Gandhi.

They can understand why certain injustices can be explained by Reincarnation. Those unfortunate ones are really more fortunate than millions in our country. Why has reincarnation not been accepted in the western world?

Because, we are a Christian world, dominated not by the Law of God, but by the law of the church. The clergy still holds the spiritual strings, which it pulls when it desires. It is not in the interest of the clergy to place the fate of each one of us in our own hands.

No vicarious atonement, no belief in slogans of "Jesus saves," or that someone else's sacrifices can save our sins. The Law of Reincarnation makes each one responsible for his own actions. If they feel right, their feelings will change their attitude and the attitude of people to them. Jesus said – What you plant you reap. Plant this wind and reap a whirlwind. That was teaching reincarnation, for Jesus taught it.

He asked his disciples who men said he was. Moses, Elijah, John and others he was told. Then he asked, "Whom do ye believe I am?" Peter replied that he was the Messiah, the Anointed One, how can anyone deny reincarnation that reads the Bible?

But, reincarnation is undesirable for the masses, for then the priests could not say I place you in heaven, or hell, if you are or aren't good. A criminal, who has committed all sorts of crimes, has a change of heart at the last minute, not because of God, but from fear of a devil and gets absolution and makes his peace with God. What a surprise when he wakes up on the other side to find it isn't so at all!

If America is to carry the Torch of Liberty, not alone material but mental, human beings should not be subjected to the spell of politicians, or religions, or friends, or even a husband or wife.

The majority are under spells, more here than anywhere else.

Someone eats a gold fish and everyone else has to do likewise. One boy scribbles on his slicker, and every other boy and girl has to do so, too. That is all falling under a spell. The human who falls under the spell of another human being is a weak one.

Reincarnation helps break that spell, for it puts on each of us the responsibility for our own actions. Because an individual, the finest of his time, suffered on the cross for the rejection of his teachings, because he did so much for humanity, those teachings should have been made into a part of everyone's life.

Until the 3rd century, reincarnation was taught by the Christian religion, not till after that was it discarded. Shedding his blood, and suffering his utter disappointment at his betrayal even by his own disciples, Jesus spoke of what he could do, what he suffered has to be borne by all. Yet, his suffering is made the bait to catch the ignorant today.

What logical reason, have we to accept reincarnation? If we make a mistake, especially in the case of crime, it is well known that one who performs a crime sooner or late comes back to the scene of that crime. Likewise, with a good deed, or a happy experience, we like to return to the place where we have that happy memory.

No one can solve all problems in this short span of life; yet a longer life would be a curse. The majority, want to retire, to rest at an age far less than mine. Think if they had to live through 500 years of that struggle!

The base of Reincarnation is the Law of Cause and Effect. Understanding that Law removes this reliance on prayers, wishes or money.

You will get to know your own self better than before, learn how to evade reliance on others, and how to stand on your own feet. It is fine to share with a neighbor, but nothing which anyone else can do, concerns your inner self. There is a part of your life where you take no advice or counsel from others; you find within yourself the proper answer.

Try to do your best and often you get the cold shoulder. You will learn that probably somewhere or time before you started the cause, which brought about that effect.

We must go on and on till the last mistake is corrected, the last veil removed. Then only will happiness be ours. Happiness, which is not earned, is not deserved, and the thing not deserved is not enjoyed.

Not only we, but events reincarnate. I have not been talking to your for the first time. Maybe we have met many times before. I, the one to explain and others to listen. Born in many countries, yet here we are gathered together. Again, some will join, others won't be interested. Still again we will be reborn and again gather, and so on.

Reincarnation works in every department of life, for it is the means by which mistakes can be corrected.

THIRD FRIDAY ASSEMBLY
April 1945

Dear Friends and Fellow Lightbearers,

For two months, now, we have not had a General Assembly, but received a class given by Svetozar in its place. You were not told about the passing of the Light the month before, so it will be told this month.

Third Friday, in March 1945: Svetozar gave the Esoteric meaning and explanation of the Passing of the Light. Clara B. passed the Light to one of our oldest students, Katherine B. Svetozar stood behind the Seat of Inspiration with arms folded as this action took place. It so happened that a few drops of oil dropped on to the Chair during the passing of the Light as indicating the Anointment of the Blessed. Spreading a pure linen handkerchief over the oil, Svetozar seated himself, and began the wonderful explanation of the Light. No one took notes, so this account is from the memory of one of the students.

"In Eternity, the Great Law gave the Light to Lucifer, with these words, *'This Light is given to you in all Love and Joy; bear it to the world in the same Spirit that you receive it, and its Glowing Flame shall wax in radiance to the Empyrean of Eternal Light'*. With these words glowing within him, he gave this message to the Lightbearers of this world, to carry them through the darkness into the Light of Understanding.

Never before in the history of mankind has such government been expressed. As each student Lightbearer receives the Light, that student becomes the Leader of Humanity with FULL POWER to express Supreme Leadership. No Government or Country has ever given this honor to the common individual. As we are all Sons of the Great All, for the moment we are given the Divine privilege of leading our Brothers toward the Light.

The Lightbearers have established on the material plane, the Harmonious form of Government; thus establishing at the beginning of the Sixth Cycle, the New Era of the pattern of Divine Rule, on Earth as it is in Heaven. This Great Privilege has such a deep Spiritual meaning that the student bearing the Light is carrying out the most Sacred Duty.

As each different faith looks for the Savior or Messiah of their own belief, The Lightbearers have already established on Earth, the very things they are still looking for. Jesus walked the Divine Road ALONE, and it is given to each Lightbearer to carry on. We are endeavoring to blaze the trail expressed on this Earth by Jesus, by living and expressing the Will of the Father; on Earth, the Material Plane as it is in Heaven, the Spiritual Plane.

In order to do this each and every one of us must overcome the Three Temptations. So, for the first time in humanities history, the explanation was given to the World Center of the Lightbearers, and with humility the student will, as nearly as possible, relate it to you.

Jesus never gave an account of his experience in the Wilderness with the Three Temptations. So, no one ever knew what they consisted of, until it was given to one through Inspiration, to tell but not explain the experience which enabled Jesus to walk the Divine Road. This one was inspired thus in order to pass it on to humanity for its own unfoldment. Only now for the first time has the explanation of these Three Temptations been available, and until we pass the test of each one, we will have to keep coming back until we learn these lessons.

First Temptation – It is the common error of humans to give material needs and desires precedence over Spiritual needs and desires. This is fundamentally wrong, because Spirit must always come first. It is natural thus, and very un-natural to try to live any other way. But, because we are humans we have turned every natural Law backwards. So, the first Temptation is to be overcome by example of the experience of Jesus.

Jesus was tested with hunger in the wilderness. His first impulse was to use his knowledge of Universal Life Energy to manifest food for his human self, but the overcoming of the first temptation was to realize the first need was food for the soul. Communion with the Father being first, in the wilderness, sacred place of the most High, the hunger of all other needs will be supplied.

Svetozar experienced his first temptation by being placed in the position of material need, not only for himself, but for his mother also. During this time an opportunity to hold a position which would enable him to realize some of his fondest dreams was given him. The temptation was great because so much could be done towards the building of schools and colleges for the teachings of the Science of Being. His Mother who was so dear to his heart would have the things in life she deserved. But, he wanted to teach and could not do both.

There is a saying in Russia, "The morning is wiser than the evening." So, he told the man who tempted him with worldly success, that he would give him his answer in the morning. After weighing the one against the other, he realized that he should trust the Great First Law. His answer was "no."

As a result, though it did not come all at once, the Great Law took care of him at every turn. And, today he has surrounding him the utmost in beauty and quality, amidst the most harmonious Vibrations; with the chosen ones to teach and as channels through which all of Humanity can be reached. Many were called, but few were chosen.

As Easter is almost here, nine days away, a new Government is born. The Resurrection means rebirth. While all of the Christian World is greeting this occasion, The Lightbearers are giving Birth to the first Physical manifestation of True Government on Earth, at the beginning of the sixth cycle of humanity's evolution.

The Second Temptation came to Jesus in the form of the human mind urging him to prove his Power by throwing himself from the temple roof; if he remained unharmed, it would prove to his fellow beings that this Power he possessed was greater than anything else. But, after thinking this over, he realized that the desire to test the Great Law was only doubt in the very essence of life itself. So, he used and trusted the Power. Thus, overcoming the second temptation.

Svetozar has been overcoming the second temptation by refusing to exploit Universal Life Energy and his knowledge of it for proof to the doubting ones. The Great Law can test the doubters, but the doubters can never test the Great Law. Universal Life Energy is to be first manifested on Earth, and then all other things will be added unto us.

The Third Temptation is the choice of Two Roads, Human and Divine. Jesus was offered the leadership of the Jewish people if he would follow the old way, but Jesus knew that only by blazing the Divine Road on Earth, could he fulfill his mission to humanity. So, he walked alone on Earth to show the way it is done in Heaven. What he did, we must do also. By using Universal Life Energy and going into the Wilderness, (The Higher self,) to meet the Three Temptations, we shall as Lightbearers to the World blaze the Divine Road on Earth as it is in Heaven, for His Kingdom and Glory.

Svetozar in his Strength and Wisdom, teaching the Laws and loving us enough, ready to be damned for Eternity, if need, to pay the penalty of leading his brothers the wrong direction, has and is living the Four Square Principle. But, first comes the USE of Universal Life Energy. Without it the Four Square is the letter only. With IT, it becomes Spirit expressed on Earth.

Religions have veiled the Truth to gain human power, and now Svetozar has in our presence, condemned and damned the religious beliefs and teachers that have retarded the growth of humanity.

It is the most Sacred thing on Earth to bear the name Lightbearer. The six-pointed Star, our emblem, begins to reign on Earth. By establishing these teachings on Earth, we are liberating humanity from the shackles that have held them for millions of years in Ignorance and Fear. It is an established fact on Earth, because we are accepted and recorded by man made laws in Washington, D.C., Our Constitution is registered and established, Our Text Book copyrighted, and the Organization functioning.

This is why it is so important for every member to assemble as often as possible, as we are the human channels through which the Power of Universal Life Energy will reach suffering Humanity. "FOR THE PROTECTION OF THE GOOD, FOR THE DESTRUCTION OF EVIL DOERS, I AM BORN FROM AGE TO AGE," is the message of Love to suffering Humanity. *Science of Being, Pg. 128.*

Lesson given by the Baron Eugene Fersen
May 25th, 1945

"The main objective is to help bring about Humanity's Evolution through Science."

The reason we use the word Science in connection with Evolution is because Science is supposed to be organized knowledge; and Evolution is really the organized unfoldment of knowledge. We unfold through knowledge all the time; even an unfoldment, which is supposed to be instinctive, like the development of plants and the lower animals, is based on a form of knowledge called Experience.

Each experience is to a certain extent the open door to another experience, and throughout the whole of eternity there will be continually new experiences following one upon the other. Even when we reach the realm of Harmony there will still be something new to know and that much in proportion to gain, further unfoldment.

If we were as infinite in our knowledge or actual expression as is the Infinite we could not advance. In order for the Law of Evolution to work, there must be the possibility for us to grow. The Eternal having reached the limit is yet in a way evolving also, through us, through the whole universe. For the Eternal there is nothing more to do, for all there is in the Eternal; hence it evolves through us. Our evolution is our unfoldment through the Life of the Eternal.

Astronomers speak of an expanding Universe. I am not going to go into the details as to why they claim that, but the Universe cannot expand, for how could that which is All expand? If All is All, then it must include all expansion possible; within the All, parts can expand, but the Whole cannot be more than the Whole.

The Universe is limitless like time is without end. How can the Limitless expand? Within the Limitless Universe, the worlds can expand; the stellar systems can expand. What is more correct is that our knowledge of the universe expands, in proportion as our knowledge expands, as does our consciousness. The more we know; if what we know is in the right direction, the more our consciousness expands.

The Eternal, to balance itself manifests the Universe. For the Law of Cause and Effect demands an Effect for every Cause, hence there cannot be only one pole Cause, and nothing to balance it. There must be Substance to balance Spirit. The tangible Matter or Substance is the expression of the intangible Spirit. The Manifest is the evidence of the Unmanifest. The Eternal, immovable, expresses through perpetual motion, and the Eternal completion expresses itself through the incomplete expanding eternally.

The Law of Evolution is according to the Law of Harmony, the completion of the Great Law. The Great Law has its own pole in the Law of Evolution. The Great Law includes all Laws including the Law of Evolution, but if we call the Law of Harmony a pole having the Law of Evolution as its opposite, then the Law of Harmony and the Law of Evolution with all other Laws make up the Great Law.

The Law of Harmony without advancement would become stale throughout Eternity. The perfect must be ever expanding, and this can only be achieved through the Law of Evolution, of growth.

Evolution develops through Science, through knowledge, for without knowledge there could be no evolution. We have experiences and each one becomes the stepping stone to a higher experience. The highest form of evolution is to unfold and to know that you are unfolding. The first stage of evolution is instinctive, we are unaware of our unfoldment, next in line is the awareness of our growth, and finally we can deliberately press on in the line of growth we choose.

We do not evolve through Love, but through Mind. Throughout eternity mind must evolve, though not the mind of the Eternal for that is complete.

In the not so distant future, for instance, we will probably be able to talk the languages of birds, of animals, of everything. The trees talk, for that idea of the Druids about the language of trees is not wrong; they do talk and say plenty. That will all be a part of our expansion.

Second Lesson

"There motto is: 'Know thyself and thou shalt know all.'"

This is a very old saying, and highly regarded, especially by the Greeks who laid stress on knowledge. So important that they had it carved in marble over the entrance to their temples.

It is through evolution of one's own mind that knowledge is increased, and the more we throw the Light within ourselves, the clearer we see things without.

We must be ourselves enlightened before we can enlighten others. Self-knowledge is the greatest knowledge; yet how few today realize that. We take so little trouble to study ourselves. There are thousands of scientists who study everything from worlds as a whole to microbes and don't know anything about themselves. The majority that study outside phenomena know hardly anything of themselves.

If human beings would study themselves, that self-knowledge would give them the key to all else. As it says in the Bhagavad Gita – "the greatest science is the science of self." If human beings through their highest representatives could have tried to know themselves, humanity would not be today a bunch of "could-be's," but "aren'ts."

That is why we have that motto, for it explains exactly the Science of Being, it explains the aim, the means and the law through which the aim is achieved. It shows us the start and gives us an idea of the finish. It is the most wonderful statement, which any human being could utter, and in taking the best of everything to join into one harmonious whole, we naturally took it.

"The message of THE LIGHTBEARERS to the world is:

'Express in every act of yours All Energy, Intelligence, Truth and Love…'"

We had to condense in a very few words our message – not what we believe, but what we want others to know. It is great to believe but it is greater to share that belief in the form of knowledge.

Religions have creeds, the word means I believe, not I know, for they never dared to say I know. We know – we do not claim to know all, there is only One who knows all, the Eternal. No one else will ever know all, but we will always be in the process of knowing more of all. What we know we want to share, for we are not Lightkeepers, but Lightbearers.

The very activity expressed in the word shows the principle of sharing, which is an eternal principle. Our Father shares his Life, Intelligence, Law and Love with us. Our Father gives us exactly fifty percent of everything; that is why we should give fifty percent to the world, if we wish to be like the Eternal. That is why fifty-fifty appeals so to us, it is an Eternal condition.

The Universal, the Eternal created us in the exact tangible counterpart of its intangible nature. Fifty-fifty, fifty plus fifty makes one hundred, one with countless O's symbolizes Eternity; the Eternal backing up its unity.

We don't say the word to believe and be saved, we TELL them, which is entirely different.

The word is the first activity of our Father – Express. We could not know there is a Father but for his expression. No credo ever starts with that for no blind belief can be scientific. In the first word we unite ourselves with the Eternal Activity. Express – don't hold back.

How can we reconcile that first word with, 'I thought of talking, but was afraid they wouldn't understand…' Is that expressing? Remember, Express has two strange letters at the beginning and end – E and S. There is a whole world in that one word Express: E for Eternal and S for Savior.

The Eternal is the Savior – the only Savior – there is no other. In that first word you have the whole of our Teaching, of our attitude included, and also you have me, the Messenger today: E for Eugene and S for Svetozar.

You see, my friends, if you only knew how much you have in every word of that constitution; how much there is of secret meaning, how many potent symbols. Our book and constitution cannot be read; they must be studied and pondered, then only will you understand how sacred is our constitution. This is the constitution for the whole of Humanity, for those here on Earth and for those no more, for the visible and the invisible worlds.

"In every act of yours…"

Here is the word "In." I spoke to you of those who are out, we say to the world – In. We don't want them out - we want them In - included in that circle of Light, of every increasing luminosity. Inside sacred walls, not outside, is where they belong. It is only human beings who deliberately put themselves outside.

That is why when the disciples of Jesus, with the exception of John, deserted him, they went outside the inner circle of teachings and never got back. No matter how they regretted, how they tried to atone they could not, and this is why each one of them died a violent death. Religions try to hold their deaths in martyrdom as a credit to them, but those deaths showed the Great Law had discredited them. The only one who remained faithful, John, died a normal death. There is proof that the Great Law credited John, but discredited the unfaithful.

That is why the teachings of Jesus have been so perverted, because all except John had lost their place in the inner circle and could not regain it no matter how they tried. John begins his Gospel with the Word of the Eternal, not with Jesus. That is why the Religion of today is not the Religion of the Apostles, or of Jesus. The best that is in it can be traced to Paul, who was not a disciple of the living Jesus, but who never betrayed him. He never heard the Teacher, however, and could only repeat from hearsay.

What a tragedy…If only those disciples would not have place themselves *Out*, there probably would have been true Religion on Earth; but those first channels closed themselves. We tell Humanity you are *In*.

"Every Act…"

"Every" comes from ever, standing that is for Eternity. We are all supposed to be in for eternity. We will none of us reach Harmony until the last one through countless incarnations will be born again In and stay In. The majority are born in, but at the end of their life find they have stayed out.

You have no idea how sad it is to be able to perceive things as I do. To see people on the street, young and old and to say – Out, out, out, out, in, out, out, out, in – It is terrible, because you do not want to feel so many are out, and so few are in. They are our brothers, our companions; co-prisoners in that concentration camp of the subconscious, surrounded by the barbed wire of our own short comings.

Sometime the day of liberation will come, but not yet, for we are still under the rule of the world. It is sad indeed to see so many out, and so few in.

Act – without activity there can be no life, for life is activity, motion is the first corner of the Four Square. Be active forever in every direction. Be true to that principle of life expressing through activity, in the physical place, by activity on the mental plane, and by activity on the spiritual plane, by threefold activity.

"Of yours…"

That message is to the world, and because we give it to the world it is supposed to be theirs. We do not say "ours" but "yours." We should always remember that though we are students of Science of Being, we are teachers to the world. It is therefore our privilege to say "yours" and not "ours."

It is a sign of modesty; you place them in their own eyes ahead of you. If one says "ours," one puts oneself first and others next; when one says "yours," one puts others ahead, to each one he is first.

If human beings would realize the direct connection of their acts with their being, there would be an entirely different life on earth. They don't realize each act they express remains connected to them energetically, and will always come back.

As in that statement – No thought, no feeling, no action good or ill is ever lost. Soon or late it will come back.

If only human beings would realize that connection between themselves and their acts, physical, mental acts and thoughts, emotional acts and feelings.

"All Energy..."

We start the most beautiful sentence by the name of the Eternal. *All* is the beginning and *All* is the end. Three letters, symbolizing the trinity of the Eternal, lay the foundation, the standard of the Eternal. Thou art All; and in the name of All we start everything we do.

Energy – again a word of power. E is the letter of the Eternal. A strange letter E, the top reaches down and the bottom reaches up; the Eternal looking at humanity and humanity looking at the Eternal, with mind a little outgrowth between. But, some day they will expand, and form a Four Square, when men will reach God. That is the greatest symbol of the Eternal, the Four Square. Mind is represented in the E, by the incomplete cross.

"Intelligence..."

Starts with an *"I"* symbol of the Eternal *"I."* *"I"* stands for unity with the Eternal, and the ending letter E again stands for the Eternal. Through our unity with the Eternal, we become one with the Eternal.

That *"I"* united with the Eternal, where all knowledge is placed by and by at our disposal. I say 'Let there be Light,' and the very end gives a feeling of security. I am the One who gives Life Eternal.

"Truth and Love..."

Truth has a peculiar value today through the number of letters. T is the symbol of God, Theos, and five letters symbolize the Four Square with the point of a pyramid. That is as much as Humanity is permitted to realize of truth today. Someday the simpler word – *Law*, will be used. Law is simpler, it has only three letters, three is the number of Divinity, while five is the number of present day humanity. When we have learned, as humans, the Truth, we will realize that the Truth is the Law, then we will read Truth as Law. You have always heard me say Truth or Law.

Law and Love, which are on the other side of Life and Mind, are one. There can be no Law without Love, for Law must attract not repel. 'You shall know the Truth, and Law shall set you free.' Knowledge means union with the thing you know; even physically this holds as 'Adam knew Eve, his wife…' meant he was attracted to her, and they became one physically. Knowledge means attraction; Knowledge of Law with the attraction of Love forms the foundation of Harmony.

"And Love…" There we have the word, 'And.' The moment you say 'and' it shows a continuity, for there is no full stop when there is an 'and' used. 'And,' stands for continuity of Life, it binds together, harmonizes, that is why it is used.

The continuity between Truth and Love is there expressed. So far, people have thought that Law and Love couldn't be connected, for those who study the laws, lack the connecting link of 'and.' We say I and my friend, I and my wife, and feel the connection. When we say *I and my Father*, we see the eternal line connecting. It is a powerful word, that is why it is not used for the first part, but only with – *and Love*.

That is to show that humanity has not reached Love, at best they are grouped in the three corners of the Four Square. When they have proved faithful and true in those three corners, then they can go to the fourth. No one can love who is untrue, no one can love who is dishonest; no one can love who is a liar. They may have emotions, but those feelings are a mere mockery of Love, a caricature of love. No true love can lie. A man that lies in that moment, he cannot love.

Religions and well-wishers, especially, put so much emphasis on Love, think they can reach the Eternal through love. It is possible to love an individual at a distance, but he can only be reached through the other three corners. We can love our fellow beings and should, but we should *express* our love to our fellow beings, corner of Life; we should be wise in that expression, corner of mind; and we should be sincere, and honest in relation to our fellow beings, corner of Law. Love is constant, is known by loyalty, symbolized by Law.

A human being cannot be loving if they are not loyal. We have to work out all three corners before we are fit to lay our treasures in the fourth corner of Love. That is why I do not teach Love. We can learn Energy, Wisdom and Sincerity; can learn them mentally and that is the only way; and the shortest and easiest way after all. It is only the limitation of our human mind, which thinks that it is too hard a road to walk. That is the lie within us that speaks – that lie we call the human subconscious.

Finally, *Love* the culmination of everything, the Eternal union with the source of Love. It is the last word, which when reached becomes the first. The last shall be first and the first shall be last, as was said before. When we have reached completeness with Love, then we will love, love most sincerely, love most wisely, and love with all our energy, with the wholeness of our being. Therefore, life will become last when we reach love. The order we have today to follow will be reversed.

That will be all tonight…One more word – We start our Four Square with E, for Energy, and finish with E, the last letter of Love. We are within Eternity, that Four Square is eternal.

Notes of the Baron Eugene Fersen's Lecture by L. Anciaux
February 1st, 1946

*"Express in every act of yours all Energy, Intelligence,
Truth and Love."*

The last word – Love – although most thought of in a certain way, is the one most desired and yet the least understood. Very few people understand the meaning of even the word Love; much less do they know anything of the Power back of that word. For the word is after all but the temporary expression of something which is Eternal.

Every word we use is a temporary concept of a reality far beyond human understanding of it. Each word can have a superficial or a deep meaning depending on the individual use of it; but is mere sound in the majority of cases.

Yet, the Word was with God, and the Word was God. Everything that which was made was made through the Word, for the Word the Fiat, the Commandment, "Let there be Light." It is the expression of the Unmanifest, the Effect of the Eternal Great and Mysterious Cause – Our Father.

If it is difficult for us to analyze the mystery behind a word, it is far more difficult to understand the Power of which the word is in expression.

Love being such an all embracing word, stands for an infinitely greater Power back of it; and if we are to attempt to analyze it, all we can do is analyze what the word is, the Power is beyond human understanding now.

There are so many interpretations of Love, because it is most difficult to understand even human Love, in our present state of consciousness.

We are triune beings at present – Life, Mind, and Law – combined in one – and belong to three dimensions at best. The majority of people do not even understand these yet, and are hardly more than one-dimensional. Mind is one dimensional to start, single tracked, and expands as it learns its lessons.

Mind was first as in the condition of a cloud. For a cloud there is only one certain purpose, to produce rain, there is no other value to the cloud, when the cloud condenses we have rain or snow. Similarly, with the human Mind, as it begins to condense, it forms single drops.

As normal growth proceeds, the single tracked Mind becomes broad-minded and finally deep-minded – wise. That is as far as anyone can go now, for after that, comes the Fourth Dimension, which is outside human comprehension; and in the corner of the Fourth Dimension is located Love. There is the shrine where the Power of the Infinite is represented in its Greatest Aspect.

Love being Number 4 includes also 1, 2 and 3. It is the Law and the fulfillment of the Law, for only in Love can we find both the Cause and Effect manifested in One – Completely. Only in Love can be found that marvelous Divine Rule of Multiplication. Because multiplication is represented today by the sign - X – and X also is symbolizing the Unknown, the Mystery of the Eternal, we can understand why Love is the Greatest Mystery.

Because of that, the greatest sorrows we have in life come through our misunderstanding of Love. How can we understand Love properly? We can't, for to understand that which is outside the human range of perception is impossible. When we didn't have powerful telescopes with which to explore the vastness of Space, many things we saw in the firmament at night were mysteries. The more we are able to expand our powers, to investigate, the more we are able to push away the limitations and extend the range of our understanding. We can see millions of light years into Space now, only because we have the means to do so.

If you wish to explore the ground, you have to have a tool, a spade or even the hands, with which to dig. Today we use all kinds of scientific tools to do that exploring, but the principle is the same.

Can we at present penetrate into the corner of Love? No! We are outside it, and no human being in the Third Dimension can enter into the corner of Love, The Fourth Dimension, we haven't the tools yet. What we are now forging is the tool with which to dig into that corner.

The spade will work properly only if its material is of the right kind; it must be homogeneous and strong. We have to amalgamate the three corners to make a perfect spade, with our Will Power as the handle; by which that spade is used. For we cannot properly use a spade without a handle.

Our Will Power is that handle, and we have to use it. That is why it is so important to develop our Will Power in order to make use of that wonderful tool, the triangle, to dig into the ground of Love. *Love is not the seed; it is the ground in which the seed is planted.* Love is represented by Mother Earth.

The Earth was born first, and then later on seeds were formed. The chemical elements in the Earth being those needed by the seed in order to grow. The Earth chemically speaking is our Mother. If we take loving care of the Earth, it produces wonderful results, if we neglect it we get only weeds.

We cannot abuse the Earth and escape the consequences. It has been estimated that seventy-five percent of the cultivated land in the US today has already been ruined, offering a major problem for the coming generation to correct that condition. The urge so many have today to go back to the country is because they are unconsciously attracted by the *need of the Earth for care*, and this is how the Great Law works to bring that care where needed.

It is the same with Love. There was a time when people loved in an instinctive way. Being in the corner of Life, those primitive people were closer to the corner of Love than we are today. For we start with Love in going around the Four Square, and end with Love. The Power of Attraction existed before Life. The ancient Greeks said of Eros, the God of Love, that he was the oldest of the Gods, and yet an eternal youth.

In days gone by people were more or less instinctively expressing Love, were loving, yet unaware of it, but since we can't appreciate something we are unaware of, we had to go through ages of awakening for the mind to become aware. As Mind was developed there started to come the realization of Law, when Law is brought into the fullest expression in our lives, then will we enter the Age of Love.

We cannot enter the Age of Love unless we've prepared the triangle of Life, Mind, and Law. *No human being can enter the Realm of Love*, who has not passed through those preparatory stages. That has never been explained before on this planet, for the Four Square was always a mystery, the revelation for the few, but a secret to the masses. Yet, human beings always instinctively realized *that Squareness is important*, for they used it in every direction though without understanding the power of it.

Brutal Power came first, then the cold light of Mind, and last, Law, which should mean Liberation, but Ignorance aroused Fear. Humans are afraid of complications, unconsciously they sense that a Law of Nature cannot be fooled, cannot be bargained with or whitewashed. Human beings do not realize that they should not compromise, and yet they do so all the time.

That is why Humanity has not and cannot enter into the Sacred Realm of Love. We can only prepare by adjusting the other three corners; must learn to be optimistic, to see the negative yet say, that in spite of the wrong, *we can try to do right*. It is the logical process of Unfoldment.

Unfortunately, those who are in a position to lead, not understanding Love, do more damage in trying to teach Love than do those who don't try to teach Love. They claim that the wrong is not so bad, instead of rising above it. All those who were the true Friends of Humanity – the bigger or lesser ones – they all insisted on one thing necessary for success in life – Wisdom. Wisdom, often called Common Sense, means a balanced sense. They realized that unless human beings try to be wise – to be three dimensional, they could not succeed in anything. The more you go to the Law, the deeper you go in developing your mind, and at the bottom of your Mind you realize the Law and the value of the Law. That is Wisdom.

When Law is expressed more and more in our life, when we become closer and closer to it, we realize that *"Not my will, but Thy Will be done."* As we grow in that depth of Law we find at the bottom of it, Love, the greatest manifestation of Law and its fulfillment.

There are not short cuts across the plane of the Four Square. We have to go through all those other corners; those numbered 1, 2, and 3 in order to reach the 4th. We must follow that path; yet so rare that we call it wisdom. Often among the uneducated we find Wisdom, for Wisdom does not depend on education. Tolstoi, who liked to live among the peasants did so because he found wisdom among them which he never found among his own people, because they figured things out through experience.

In former days, the Wealth and progress were built by the younger generation using the Experience and Wisdom of the older. That is not the modern way of thinking, and we in America have exaggerated that to the nth degree; we have become a people who absolutely disregard wise advise, especially if it comes from the elders.

But, humans are going someday to learn their lesson, and it will be a mighty hard one. The True Friends of humanity were wise; they were so close to Love, that they were illuminated in its glowing rays.

As we start to go around the corner of Law, we begin to perceive Love, but not until then. From behind the limitations of the three dimensional world we begin to see that Sun of Love rising, and its rays will embrace and guide us as we approach the Fourth corner until we become One with it. The Wisdom, which lies at the bottom of Law, is already illumined by the Sun of Love.

The Moon has no power of light in itself, its light is all derived from the Sun; that light is modified, made more gentle, yet it has a tremendous effect on the Earth. The Sun is the power back of the Light; the Moon is the corner on which the Sun Shines.

It is the same as we approach Wisdom, for the corner of Law is "THE LIGHTBEARER." We, the Lightbearers, are now starting to teach from the corner of Law, leaving the corner of Mind to the scientists. For we are now fulfilling that prophecy of 2000 years ago, "The Eternal Father will send you the Holy Ghost, the Spirit of Truth, Law which will teach you all things." Jesus could never have said, "I will send," for that would have put him above God. Who can send the Great Law but the Eternal? Jesus knowing that always said, "I can do nothing of myself, but what the Father does I can do also."

We Lightbearers are fulfilling that prophecy in the corner of Law. We are like the Moon reflecting the Light from the Sun of Love to the Earth; we give that Light we receive to Humanity and it is continually replenished. We are the Moon to Humanity, sending them the gentle Light into the Darkness of Today, to make it less dark.

We are doing our work until the day comes when a greater Work will be done, not by humans or organizations, but by the Eternal Himself. The next Great Teacher will be our Eternal Father. He is the Greatest Teacher; and we teachers small or great receive what He taught us, and hand it over to the World, subdued, gentle, and appropriate to the times.

The Moon Light is sufficient for the Night, but when *The Day* will come then the Sun will be the ruling power, which will embrace all the world in the warm folds of its Love. Moon rays are cool, not freezing us, but also not scorching us, as would the rays of the Sun; they are gentle, as symbolized by the gentle flame of our Light of Inspiration.

That explains why human beings have so much trouble in loving. As humans cannot really love, as they should, the best they can do is to express it in a subdued way – a friendly way. Goodwill is the finest expression today of Love. It does not seek anything for its own use; it is generous.

Even Lovers begin to love because they can gain from and give to each other, and then the realization takes place and they discover something missing. Fortunately, life is so generous, that in spite of that disappointment, something takes place to compensate that disappointment, and a child is born. There again the greatest opportunity is given to express Goodwill to the child.

But, Goodwill is not shown to the child, who is pampered by its parents for the sake of their vanity; usually it is the vanity of the parents that makes them want their child to grow in body and mind, not the sound interest in their child's welfare.

How can we talk of Friendship? Today people are friends, tomorrow – enemies. Humans have to learn the lesson of Love, and it is the last because it is *the most important* and the hardest lesson of all. We are amongst the few who teach it the proper way, we the Lightbearers also have it clearly defined in our Commandment. Love, the last corner, makes out of the triangle that wonderful figure "The Four Square," Eternal Harmony.

*

(Closing remarks addressed to Harold L., Presiding Lightbearer)

In a way the Men need the lesson of Love more than do Women. Women are the embodiment of Love; for they are the ones who countless ages ago realized their original mistake of Separation from the Eternal and were willing to take through millions of years a secondary place in order, by and by to correct that mistake.

Men belong to that group of Beings who through their stubbornness refused to admit their mistake. That is why it is so essential for Men to realize that lesson of Love.

You, in the Seat of Inspiration represent The Lightbearers, while I am in the Seat of Silence. Through you, I am reaching the whole of Humanity, including the young men and women of the younger generation. It is a message of Hope, for if they will do the right thing, they shouldn't worry about the Future.

Six Lessons given by the Baron Eugene Fersen
October 1947 through March 1948

"Because even love must be manifested on the material plane…"

Some expressions are just a gentle look, but it is a look of material eyes. Some are a gentle word – it is a word, but it sounds on the material plane. Some a gentle gesture, but it is a gesture expressed through the material body. Some people think it is enough for them to feel that all inside and never manifest it outside, but that does not mean building. BUILDING MEANS MANIFESTING.

Therefore, remember our acts are to be on the material plane manifested thought. The source is not only the mental plane but some acts have their source in the Spiritual Plane, yet they must be manifested on the material plane.

Every human being should manifest in their own way. We should not ape anybody. Others' fine acts should be an inspiration to us, but we should never copy them or ape them. The moment we copy and ape we are no longer manifesting anything of our own and we cannot manifest anything, which is not our own because that would mean stealing on the mental plane. We are then unconscious thieves on the mental plane.

We rob somebody else of their good traits and we clothe ourselves with that. It is a very subtle thing, which very few people realize. We have among religious literature no end of books on the imitation of Jesus. That phrase, "to be like Christ, or Christ-like," is nothing but an invitation to imitation, and imitation is not a genuine product. It is a substitution, a stand in, where the actual one who does it has no reward for it but is considered by the Great Law a mental thief. What we explain in the Science of Being is the very reverse of what Humanity generally accepts.

That is why we are continually misunderstood. We should not pay any attention to that misunderstanding. Now it says, "TO BUILD," to what? The building should give freedom. The more we build our body, the stronger, the freer we are; the more we build our mind in the right direction, the wiser we are, and freedom and wisdom are synonymous. The more we manifest our acts on the physical plane, expressing in a line, which interests us – to make money, the freer we are. There is nothing greater than right acts and building.

To build means to create, and the Eternal is the Great Creator. We are the children of the Eternal and the first thing is to create, and we call that building. By building we create the first thing most indispensable, and that is freedom.

Now the word freedom itself is the most misunderstood and misused word on this planet because human beings, except a few, consider self-will freedom and it then becomes license. Self-will is no freedom. It is the greatest enslavement we can put upon our own mind, upon our own conscious self by the tyranny of The Subconscious.

Freedom is not based on the material things only, freedom is the Eternal state and condition of our Soul, and in that condition, naturally, we cannot humanly perceive in all its fullness. But, when we do create a work by doing that which any insect can do, every animal can do, a bird can do – they all build. And, the result of that creative urge manifested on the material plane is first noticeable in an increasing sense of true freedom. Then we need strength, because of what use to us is freedom if we are not strong enough to make use of it. Of no use at all.

November 1947

Therefore, as we want to get the fullness of life we must be strong enough to enjoy that fullness. That is why in days gone by, when naturally people were primitive and sometimes crude in their ways of thinking and living, the weak ones, the sick ones, the crippled ones, were utterly disregarded. That was not unnatural because Mother Nature, as I have told you so often of all things is the least impressed by weakness.

In other words – the survival of the strongest and we human beings naturally being children of Nature have since time immemorial tried our best to keep that Law of Nature the best we humanly can. You may say, "But, to take care of the weak, of the sick, of the suffering, of the poor, is a wonderful problem." It is wonderful if our intention is to make the sick healthy, to help the weak to gain strength, and to help the poor to get on their feet financially. It is beautiful to do the corrective thing, but it is still more beautiful and reasonable, if we use the preventive cure – not the corrective.

Some day it will come. There is a general tendency in that direction. We usually do not prevent the thing because of our human shortsightedness. We usually do not see and do not want to see that which is beyond our immediate problem. Obviously, we have to take care of the immediate problem, but we have all the future to look at too, to make the immediate problem full of realizations in the right direction when the future will become the present.

Therefore, remember, as I so often have told you, build your own strength, but also remember our human strength is not measured by the amount of pounds we can lift, though it is to a certain extent important too, but remember that our greatest burden is to start with a mental burden, and among the mental burdens we have to carry the hardest burden of all for each one of us is The Subconscious. It is a terrible burden.

It is there where our human self, which we call as its best, the conscious self, should learn to grow strong, and that is what the majority of people absolutely fail to understand. That is where unfortunately we have the secret of the deterioration of the whole of the human race in this age. The whole race passes through a process of deterioration because we have no strength manifested, yet, to fight our own lower self.

Every teacher, even in the primary, in the high schools should have, as foremost aim for those who come to them for instruction, to help them to develop what is called the strength of character. As I so often mentioned to you, that character of ours is the most precious thing we possess. It has more worth than anything else on earth – more worth than all the recognition of the world, more worth than material honors, more worth than ordinary knowledge, that is, what we gain through ordinary books, to know how to do this and do that. *Self-knowledge is Supreme.*

Through analyzing our own self we help to build the strength of our own character, remember we are free to do that. We usually make alibis and say to our own selves – "I am handicapped to do that by this or that…" Some of our surroundings are handicaps, but that should not stop the building of our character. On the contrary, that should increase the strength of our character if we would build, in spite of the handicaps.

December 1947

Trees that are exposed to strong winds have much stronger roots than those that are not exposed to them. Use the Law of Analogy. Wind on the material plane is an indication of what is happening on the mental plane. Do not be satisfied with that excuse, "poor thing," – that person has been brought up in surroundings of disharmony; especially since in most homes there is no harmony. Seeming happiness which you find in some homes is nothing but the form of self-defense an individual builds up as a protective measure against the disharmony of most homes.

Many mental disharmonies are not expressed yet on the material plane, but are still more dangerous and deteriorating than simple material manifestations of disharmony. Even though in the midst of disharmony, still that does not excuse us for yielding to those surroundings, and I am giving you as illustrations the tree. If it does not resist the wind it will be uprooted, yet a tree, which resists the wind will grow sturdy and strong. The reason most people are uprooted is because they have not developed the mental resistance against undesirable disharmonious surroundings. Nothing will excuse that.

It is pretty bad to be weak on the physical plane, but it is a thousand times worse to be weak on the mental plane. That is why when we act in the right direction not only act, but, as it has been explained previously – act with energy, act with intelligence, act with sincerity, and act with enthusiasm, we are bound to build in the right direction, to create in the right direction.

So, remember again, I am repeating so many things, but don't try to find for yourself that surroundings influence you to do the wrong thing. As long as you will throw that on surroundings you will never be able to look at your own self, face to face, because you throw the responsibility on your surroundings.

Just like our human mind, instead of looking at its own self and seeing all the horrible things The Subconscious has back of that human mind, we throw the responsibility either on matter, or on evil. Religious people have a still better scapegoat – the devil. That won't do. And, I know there are millions of people, especially today, who think they can get away with it. They can't. And, the sad part is that the longer they postpone it the harder it will go. There is a German saying – "What Johnny has not learned as a child, John will never learn as a grown up man!"

The older we grow the more difficult it is to gain self-control over our self. Self- control must be developed and if we do not develop that by free will, we are by and by in later years weaker physically and weaker mentally because we are disappointed. Disappointment is one of the worst mental handicaps, where we are suspicious and suspect every act of someone, suspect them to keep something in their sleeve, behind their human mind.

You know very well that the majority of people are suspicious. They are distrustful and, in a way, you cannot blame them; but when we are distrustful we are at our worst mentally and we finally end by distrusting the Eternal. How can we under such a condition of distrust, be strong? It is impossible.

January 1948

Remember when we are young we are full of trust, full of confidence, full of optimism, and that should be kept as one of our most precious assets. That does not mean that we should trust unreasonably. We should use judgment. We should know where to trust and where not to. Remember, there is a great difference between trust and distrust, and trust and not trust. Be cautious. If we simply do not trust, are cautious, we are still on the positive side. We still give the individual the benefit of the doubt, but if we distrust, it is negative – on the wrong side.

The young generation today, as a general rule, are the most distrusting beings probably who ever walked upon this earth and they cannot be blamed in a way, though they should be warned why that is all wrong. Probably their surroundings made them distrustful. Before people were too gullible and the pendulum swung in the opposite direction. Now they are distrustful.

I am speaking about building strength of character. It is difficult to succeed when we are getting old. When even sometimes in a more mature age people seemingly show a stronger character, it isn't at all their own strength which they show – it is the whip of Destiny which simply whips them to use their last forces in order to wobble through life.

It is like a race. A fine thoroughbred horse does not need any whipping – it will run and give all that it has. The horse with no character will usually lose out. Yet, sometimes such a horse will win because it is whipped, but very seldom the first prize. Now the same is with people who have not developed while they are young, their character. The Great Law will whip such an individual, not to win the race – but to race.

The Individual may be far behind everybody else but still he races, and will be continually whipped and whipped, until the end of his earthly days. Nobody can escape that – nobody should want to. If the young generation would only be interested enough in the old generation and study their lives – not only by studying successful lives which are very few, but by looking around and seeing the failure of the majority of people and saying to themselves, "No, why should I be such a failure?" It would help them, but they always think because they are young and have no experience that they can somehow avoid it. They think, "I have some fine traits which will bring me out of the mess…" No matter how many fine traits an individual has to start with, if we do not exercise those fine traits, they become shriveled. If we are kind and do not exercise kindness, we, by and by lose the kindness.

If we are strong in character and do not exercise that through acts we lose the strength. Any organ, which is not exercised, loses its power on the physical plane and it is exactly that way on the mental plane. The majority of youngsters have some very fine fundamental traits. I have known quite a number of such young men and women, but when I saw them some years later, what was the result – complete deterioration. WHY? Because they always believed that in a moment of need they could bring out their qualities, but when the need came to bring it out the quality was almost paralyzed. So, we should never rely on that.

February 1948

We have to understand life and love as they really are. To do things the best we know in the process of our Evolution. NOW is a transitory stage through which Humanity passes and the lessons to be learned from that stage is to try not to be any more perverted in the sense of true values.

Why should animals or humans be killed? Why are human beings killed? Because humans generate human beings, they feel perfectly right as they think they create life, they have the right to take life. Why are we ashamed of our human bodies? Why is the word called bodily decency so important? Why were ancient Greeks not ashamed to show bodies completely nude? Because they had a more normal sense of life…Today humans have lost it mostly because of the fundamental insurgencies of organized religion. In other words, even decency has been perverted by some organized religions. This is not living life. This is perverting life.

When we say in our Teachings, "Thus, living can you only live," we mean infinitely more. I could explain that to you for days and days, yet, it is up to you, to those of you who read our Constitution not just to take the letter, the words, but to dig into the meaning of the words deeper and deeper, even if the ground is hard, still you can dig harder to break through the ground.

Break the opposition, which you find in the Present as well as in the dead Past. Remember, in most cases the greatest opposition to be found is the Past.

A woman may be very decent today, yet, maybe in the Past she was not considered decent, according to the standard of days gone by, maybe she was not even as she herself thought she was. A thing, which is past, should not be given power to influence the Present. The Present should be strong enough to stand on it's own feet. The Present is like a new light, which should dispel every possible shadow of the Past. And, yet, Human beings say, "A woman with a past." She may be much more decent, more intelligent, more loving than one without a past.

That is perversion of Life. That, all due to the original Great Perversion which we started once and for which we pay now throughout billions of years of our existence. We will continue to pay until we have learned the proper values of Life. Human beings will be compelled, like caterpillars who ate up their leaves to migrate to better quarters, to a better life. Humanity is not bad in its own way in spite of all its foolishness, which is due to Ignorance and Laziness. Because of Ignorance, Humans have a perverted sense of Life and because of Laziness they are not even willing to make a little effort to regain that loss of the right sense of Life.

So, I trust that each time when I am explaining to you a word or passage of our Constitution it is done according to the Law of Evolution, a step toward growth, each step taking you further, steps which carry you from details through the main Fundamental Trunk, to the Very Roots of Life Itself. Those Roots, which are grounded into the Infinity of Time and Space.

March 1948

We have to learn to find balance in our own self. If we continually let the Subconscious upset that balance how can we be happy, and the best way to get that balance is to trust the Great Law. Although I do not like to talk about myself, yet I wish to state this – that because of my complete trust in the Great Law in every department of life, no matter if it concerns our teachings or if it concerns material problems, or personal ones, if I do the best, The Great Law will function for me because I will be open.

I will give you an illustration. As you know I am going to Los Angeles and naturally that trip is always expensive, especially when I start. The last time when I started to Los Angeles I didn't have enough money for the trip and The Great Law provided me with the funds through you as channels. I knew that if that idea would have come to you this time it would not have been right for me to accept it and I had no other means to provide for my journey. I was not worried about it at all. If it is right for me to go there, then the means will be forth coming in the right way, and then I received unexpectedly a considerable check from a book store, ordering such a number of "Science of Being" books and "Is There a God?" that, what I can supply will be absolutely ample to take care of my trip to Los Angeles.

Now you see how the Great Law works and it works always that way for all of us, if we trust The Great Law. And, remember if we trust the Great Law, the greatest thing in the Universe, the result is that we carry with us an atmosphere of supreme trust, and if we trust The Great Law no human being can take advantage of us.

We are always warned if somebody proves to be untrustworthy. We then feel that we cannot trust that individual. Yet, we cannot classify all people as not to be trusted because some people are distrustful, and awaken within us a feeling of distrust. You know the majority of people are in that mental condition. And, think of it – we have in our own hands the means to counteract that wholly and when we will have trusted the Great Law we will have paved the way to Happiness.

We can only enter into the realm of Harmony, into the realm of Love through the gates of Law. You know enough about the Four Square Principle to know we cannot reach the corner of Love unless we pass through the third corner of Law, and Law is the Truth.

It is very difficult for some to realize after passing through life, that it was their own handicap that made it that way. It is an incarnation lost. It is the worst thing that could happen, because the next incarnation will be harder and finally it will be so hard that not being any longer able to carry the burden they will turn to the Eternal, to the Great Law as the only help, and then trust the Great Law.

JEALOUSY, HATRED, DOUBT
Written by Eugene Fersen

Real jealousy is one of the most disintegrating elements in subconsciousness. It is very subtle, and an ever increasing poison in our mental system. It is based on fear. It can never be an incentive for anything positive.

If we are jealous of someone's possessions we really hate that individual, and want to equal his possessions. There is nothing stronger on earth than hatred. It is perverted love. Hatred lives in an individual until it consumes the individual. Reasonable competition is a very laudable form of expression. If it is based on a desire to outshine someone else it is wrong. Athletes are usually very jealous of the achievements of their competitors.

The fire of hatred is like an ordinary fire. If known in time it can be extinguished. No emotion ever starts in full force. With human hatred, if we do not stop it, it makes us lose our self. It will never stop by itself.

Greed is really the counterpart of the natural desire to grow.

Doubt is based on suspicion, lack of trust, lack of faith. Doubt paralyzes every constructive activity. Life is based on "Dare and Do." We cannot dare if we doubt our own ability.

"Who has ever seen the One Who claims to be our Father and Who is called God? True it is that every morning a Voice speaks within us – but there is none can tell whether it comes from our very selves," (Science of Being, p. 311). This was the first doubt. The result was You and me and the rest of Humanity. When doubt increases too far, one has either to kill the cause of the doubt or kill himself (*See Editor notes below for further clarification). We cannot find any other solution, except by rising above the doubt.

The contradictory power of doubt is faith. Yet, Life is very strange. We cannot have faith in everything. Faith is one of the most precious gifts we have. If we would have faith as children have, it would be so great that it would solve problems beyond unbelievable opposition. If we had enough faith we could trust the most untrustworthy individual and he could do nothing against us. It is very difficult on account of our own shortcomings.

Acts, not words, prove a thing…

*Editor's notes: When doubt increases too far, one has to either to kill the cause (make peace with the cause,) of the doubt or kill himself (which means to deny that aspect of themselves, which is death of that part of themselves on the physical plane while among the living).

A DAY OF DARKNESS AND OF LIGHT

Lecture by Eugene Fersen, Good Friday, March 25th, 1932

at

Science of Being Auditorium, Montreal

I am going to explain to you tonight the general meaning of holidays and days when certain events are commemorated. In each nation and in each race you will find that there are certain dates which are kept throughout the ages in memory of events which have left their imprint upon the consciousness of that particular race or people. These events commemorated are sometimes joyful in nature.

Today the Christian world commemorates one of the greatest events in history, in fact the greatest. Not only is this true for the Christian world, but even for the non-Christian. Every part of the world even to the remotest regions was affected by that event although unaware of its occurrence.

About two thousand years ago on a Friday, on the eve of Sabbath, that is, the day consecrated to Divinity, took place a tragedy which is far greater than humanity actually realizes even today. At that time the world as a whole was in a dire condition; there was unbelievable unrest everywhere throughout the world. Everywhere was a clash of old ideas with new, everywhere a new spirit struggled to be born and humanity sought to awaken from its age-old sleep. This urge to awaken from its slough of ignorance and fear is a recurrent phenomenon.

When such a condition occurs in the whole race, conditions are very difficult, but, as occasionally happens, when this urge sweeps the entire world then those periods become even more unendurable. People are in darkness and do not know where to turn, whom to follow or what to do to extricate themselves from the condition which after all are a direct result of their own ignorance.

Because of the operation of the GREAT LAW when such a time comes to humanity the law of demand and supply becomes operative; the conscious and unconscious cry of the masses of humanity for a teacher, for an emancipator, for a liberator, for a Lightbearer, wells up from their inmost hearts. That cry from the very soul of mankind is not uttered in audible words but it gets its answer nevertheless and the proper teacher, the one who is supposed to be the leader, the liberator, the LIGHTBEARER is born.

But, strange also when an event of such unparalleled magnitude in the history of mankind takes place, humanity as a whole never perceives such a fundamental happening at the time that it takes place. And, because they do not perceive at the right time when they do begin to grasp that something has occurred it is already too late and the opportunity has been missed.

Such opportunities have been presented to mankind an unbelievable number of times and invariably mankind has missed those opportunities. Twenty centuries ago such an opportunity was given to humanity when there was born to a very fine woman, though of modest condition, a son, who later on became the best channel for the Law of the Infinite to work through.

The Law of the Infinite always works, but it cannot work through the majority because the majority are not attuned and do not perceive their relation to the infinite. The Law can only work the way it should provided there is a channel in tune with that Law; when that channel is provided then it can manifest itself in its most glorious expression, physical, mental, and spiritual.

You see, that which we call the Spirit of Harmony, God, is so sublime in its power that human beings do not and cannot perceive it directly, but when that same Power comes through a human channel it is already modified and reduced in its glory to the capacity of human understanding and then human beings can perceive the grandeur of the Infinite in its partial aspect.

It's like this, if we on earth wish to see the various aspects of the phenomena taking place in the sun; explosions, corona streamers, sun spots, etc., we do not look directly at the sun, because our eyes would be blinded and could not see those details and though the sun is very beautiful, as a general rule our eyes cannot stand so much beauty as we are blinded. Therefore in order to carry on our investigation we must dim the light in our human perception, hence we use smoked glasses to reduce the amount of light entering the eye. Then with the reduced part of the light we begin to understand the whole.

It is just the same with the Sun of the Infinite, which shines eternally upon us, but which we cannot gaze at because people would be instantly blinded, they could not stand it. There is a very interesting passage in the Bible indicating such a possibility; it is related of Moses when he went to receive the Commandments that he begged to be allowed to see the Lord and God said, "All right you shall see me," and God passed by Moses but he lifted his mantle and covered the face of Moses because no mortal can see God face to face and live, so it was only when God had passed by Moses, that Moses was able to look at his back. There in this allegorical story is expressed what I am stating in a scientific way, that the Power of the Infinite would disintegrate any with whom it comes in direct contact, that is why all that power and glory forever dwells amidst them.

Human beings are not attuned to it and cannot perceive it except as other human beings can dilute it and enable them to perceive it by reflection as it were, because the avenue through which the glory of the Infinite passes, modifies it to the understanding of their fellows. In a way it is a wonderful provision, which shows how unbelievably foolish human beings are.

As I said, when such an avenue for Truth, for Power, for Harmony is on earth, it is not only not accepted, it is usually persecuted; it is so badly treated that it has the right to say, "Foxes have holes, but the Son of Man has no place to lay his head." In other words those avenues for Truth just wander from place to place; they cannot call any place their home.

In many cases those that did such great service to mankind were killed, some escaped, but the majority paid with their lives and twenty centuries ago such a one, such a Liberator, such a LIGHTBEARER, paid with his life through untold agony for having tried to bring to his fellows emancipation from their mistakes through knowledge of how to correct them; for having dared to lift his voice against narrow creeds against social distinctions, racial hatreds, and against capitalism. One who really wanted to help mankind to find themselves true brothers, as in reality they are.

There on the cross perished humanity's hope, killed by mankind, and now we commemorate that event and for twenty centuries we have commemorated it and people go to church and sing and cry and pray and try to revive in their hearts the sorrow of the few who understood the loss. Of what avail is it to you, of what avail is it to the majority of people, such a commemoration? It cannot make right the wrong committed twenty centuries ago. It is insincere for the simple reason that those who really suffered with their Friend that was crucified – and they were mighty few – later on realized the meaning of that tragedy and the whole of their lives were changed; they never felt the same again, which is far from the case with those who today pretend to sorrow for something which they have never understood.

For remember, the majority of people rejoiced when Jesus was crucified, it was a holiday and the clergy of that day had it marked with a red letter, for he who had been a thorn in their side, he who had called them a generation of vipers, hypocrites, and liars, had been vanquished and they said to themselves he is gone now and we have triumphed. Nor, in this moment did the ignorant crowd join the few disciples who mourned that tragedy; on the contrary, they joined the Rabbi, the Clergy, and rejoiced at the downfall of their only Friend.

It may interest you to know that the majority of people who today run to churches and pray so soulfully about the death of Jesus are those very crowds which enjoyed the sacrifice of Jesus; reborn as modern twentieth century citizens they walk the earth in bodily form today. Do not think that because the Christian religion is the only one that refused to accept reincarnation today, although they did for several centuries in the beginning, that it alters the fact that we are all born again from age to age to that school called life; until we learn our lesson it is presented to us again and again under different aspects but in the same relation and often with the same people with whom in the past we had to learn.

All of you here present, lived at the time of the crucifiction, the only difference is that probably most of you do not remember…I DO, that is why I can explain so that you can understand things of such vital importance to you.

Humanity has really to feel sorry about that which happened but not at all in the way humanity thinks it should. Humanity is supposed to feel sorry at the sufferings of Jesus, but that as I said is hypocrisy, why feel sorry today when they rejoiced twenty centuries ago? Humanity has not improved in the knowledge of his teachings to have suddenly turned, not at all; they simply do it because they have been educated by the clergy to do it.

Yet, in reality humanity has plenty of reasons to be sorry, much sorrier than they actually are about that which happened twenty centuries ago, because in crucifying the Messenger of Light, the LIGHTBEARER, on the cross they really crucified their own hope for life. It was never Jesus crucified that was to help save mankind, it was the living Christ whose mission it was to do that, not the being hanging shamefully on his cross, but the being who dared to stand upon the step of the temple and denounce the Pope of those days and show where he erred, that is where his power lies and the glory, in facing fearlessly such conditions, and not at all the crucifiction.

But, on this crucifiction was built another religion, made up of beautiful pictures, false concepts, which hid the very foundation out of which it was made. It was not in the interests of those clergy to commemorate Jesus exposing religions; that would be against their own interests, and they were mighty clever, so what did they put forward as an idea for their deluded followers? That unfortunate being hanging on that cursed tree whom they had mocked and not made a god. In so doing they have mocked God more than ever before in the history of religion. The religion of Christianity is the greatest mockery in existence, the greatest mockery of God ever known.

In other religions, the devil is the worst sufferer, but it remained for the Christian religion to give this distinction to its god. The one whose goodness and beauty of soul were a marvel to his disciples, was forsaken by all and even denied by those whom he loved, and only one, John, who adored him for himself, he only of them all had enough courage to face the multitude and the whole power of the world and follow his friend and to show to the whole world that he was not ashamed of him. Then there was his mother who believed in her son, like any other mother, there was that son of hers, flesh of her flesh, crucified and suffering untold agony, forsaken and mocked by the crowd, and a few women were also loyal, humble in birth all, one even a harlot and street woman. Amongst such as these and surrounded by a miscellaneous throng, did the Great Friend of man suffer the last suffering on the cross.

Where were the rich and powerful ones of Jerusalem? They were having tea, attending the beauty parlor or making dates with their lovers. That is what was taking place twenty centuries ago. Do you realize this? I DO, *because every minute of that tragedy is just as present with me today as it was twenty centuries ago.* What happened, the great tragedy, was not alone for one being to suffer. His crucifiction was not his great suffering for when one is called to bear the Light to man one is ready from the beginning to go through any amount of suffering for the sake of those to whom the Light is to be brought.

The real tragedy was when he saw that his sacrifice, in a way, was in vain because humanity did not understand his teachings, even would not understand his love and would not understand at all the great opportunity that the Father of man was proffering them in the name of Love through one of His children, to receive the Light which they were seeking so desperately. The tragedy of darkness of human understanding which did not allow his fellows to perceive that which he offered was the last drop in his cup so full of disappointments and when that last drop fell into the cup, then a human cry went from the human heart, "Father, why hast thou forsaken me." No, he was not forsaken but humanity was forsaken, in a way, after that, and that same humanity has the right to sorrow and cry aloud. They lost an opportunity, hence they are really crying at their own loss and not over Calvary.

He rose after that tragedy, but not as humanity thinks for he did not die. I am not going to tell you how he rose because most of you would not believe it and I have no proof to offer, but it is in any event immaterial after what had happened. It was the last page in his life as a teacher. The so called resurrection and all the subsequent details have absolutely no importance; after that tragedy the crowd and Jesus had nothing in common. He withdrew himself because he knew that his mission at that time, twenty centuries ago, was at an end.

Now, for twenty centuries, humanity has been taught to commemorate that resurrection, but I say it is an irony and entirely wrong, for if those who claim to be interpreters would have stood up and said, "It was our mistake, we did not open the door to the Truth, so let us feel sorry for our own stupidity and realize how hard hearted and narrow minded we are, let us make a resolve to be more open minded next time," if humanity would have done that, if those who dare to claim to be interpreters of God would have told the multitudes the Truth to manifest itself, what would have been our subsequent moral development?

But, humanity is not ready for it, even yet, and the reason why can be laid at the feet of the clergy of Christianity. They speak about Jesus coming on clouds all dressed in white and with his followers in white, led by Peter and with a two-edged sword proceeding out of his mouth, to judge mankind. This is just again the blind leading the blind and both are falling into the ditch and their fall into that ditch is entirely upon the shoulders of the clergy of the world and that is why, by the will of the Father, their power shall be taken away and shall be given to those who are pure before the face of God.

Remember my words, you are going to see it... It is a sad thing that humanity should be in a worse plight today than they were twenty centuries ago, for then it was but a limited condition which affected but a part of mankind, but today the whole of humanity suffers. Civilized and uncivilized without distinction, must suffer through this unbelievable agony which can be compared in a way with the agony of Golgotha.

There is a road upon which humanity must now carry its cross and nine times will they fall on that road, not being able to carry their cross any further, and yet they will have to pick it up until they reach their goal – Golgotha – the place of skulls and of abomination and there humanity will be crucified. This time not one being, but the whole of humanity, and when humanity as a whole will go through that crucifiction that for which mankind was responsible in reviling and crucifying their best friend will be expiated, but not before.

As I have told you before, there is a day of retribution coming when you will see all churches destroyed and desecrated; mud thrown at relics today believed sacred and teachings of days gone by vilified and ridiculed. In that day you will perceive that the payment of that debt is taking place. It has already started in many places today, not Russia alone by any means, and in those places they throw mud and dirt at hitherto sacred statues of so called saints. It is a sign of the times that in the Vatican City, the capital of modern Christianity, a painter has been arrested who was found making obscene paintings on the statues of the saints. It is a sign of the times that in Seville a procession of religious nature with an elaborately dressed doll representing the mother of Jesus, all decked up as a the queen of heaven, and carried on the shoulders of her devotees, was attacked and mud thrown at it. All these signs show how the Law is working and today every one who claims to interpret the will of God and belongs to any religion, is getting and will get, exactly what is coming to them.

For twenty centuries, nay more, for thousands and thousands of years the Law has been waiting, for think not that the same series of misrepresentations regarding Jesus are the only ones, before him Buddha was persecuted by the priests of his day and then deified. Buddha was the Christ of the Hindus and he was reviled and persecuted, called a heretic and they tried to destroy him, but his mission was not to die a violent death. Before him was Krishna, who like Jesus died a violent death and suffered the same persecution.

But, this time history will repeat itself in a different way, those who persecuted in the past those Friends of man and thousands who were guilty of the crime of trying to help their fellows, will now be called to the bar of Truth and everyone will get just what they deserved and when that will be done and this generation of yours will see it, then the day of sorrow for mankind will become a day of joy.

Remember, when such events as I have described will take place and they have already begun, like drops of rain before a storm, then those who assert the claim to be interpreters of the words of God, but are in reality messengers of the devil, they will call out and say, "The anti-Christ is here and the world is about to be run by the Beast," remember I say that it is they who are the anti-Christs, and because they will not acknowledge their own nature and try to throw it off upon others, they will suffer extinction.

You are living in the times mentioned in Revelations; you are in full process of fulfilling those times here and NOW. When they will say to you, "Turn to us, for only through us can you be saved," that call will go unheeded because by then the bulk of humanity will have perceived the hypocrisy and deceit of all religions, who, though they call upon the name of God, will not be answered. And, so after that day of sorrow and torment we turn to the day of joy, a day when mists will be dispelled and understanding of our true relationship to the Father, the GREAT ALL, made manifest.

Friday was never meant to be a day of sorrow, each day is just as glorious as the proceeding. There is no such thing as the Sabbath, a day set apart for Divinity. All days are of Divinity and we who study the laws of nature know that it is utterly impossible for Divinity to have rested one single instant in its glorious work. The laws of the Eternal never rest and never take holidays and if the law does not rest the Power back of the Law cannot rest and the Principle which embraces them both cannot rest either. Sabbath is a manmade conception and as long as human beings feel such a day necessary for their physical comfort, let them do as in some countries, take away the pretence of its being instituted by Divinity and call it frankly a day of rest without any religious implications.

Who lied about the Sabbath? The men of the church, and because they tried and for a time succeeded, the curse of that lie about the Sabbath is now weighing them down and is upon each of those who call themselves clergy, and that curse is a human curse because spirit cannot curse.

Those courses which issue from the man who calls himself Holy Father and curses in the name of the Father are lies; they are merely human anathema, neither has he the power of forgiveness; no lie can excuse another lie.

But, a human being can curse himself and those who deliberately deceived mankind and maintained their lies by more lies in saying that one day is more sacred than another, and is God's day, have cursed themselves. Whose days, pray, are the remaining days of the week? If we believe the logic of those same teachings then we must believe that those six days which are not God's day belong to the devil, and this is the sort of thing which people call Christian teachings.

Because of that lie and many other countless lies which have been recorded with accurate precision, greater than any so called recording angel whom they claim keeps the books of judgement, for there is a Power that registers and that Power has registered the iniquities of humanity and their misleaders, the clergy, and now those lies are weighing heavier and heavier on humanity. As a result, all religions will be washed down by their lies and you will see every word that I have said come true and there, also, is explained the reason why they will come true.

But, Friday indicates a day of joy and that day was chosen by men in so called heathen lands, who were much closer to God than Christianity is today, and they called it after the gods of joy and of light. Some of them, at least, who were close to Truth, perceived that each day is a day of joy and especially the day in which Joy lives enthroned. Friday is the fifth day and stands for the fifth day of evolution, which must be a day of joy and triumph in heaven for reaching the dawn of an enlightened era.

We Lightbearers, knowing infinitely more than the average human being, because we are today the representatives of Truth before God and man, as were those few representatives twenty centuries ago, only our number is infinitely greater and our understanding more advanced, realize why Friday has been chosen for our day of Light, our assemblies. We understand why we have no Fridays of regret; no Fridays where we pray and sorrow, but we have our Friday assemblies, a day where we grow joyful in understanding and with the help of the Great Law, we know that we shall be protected by that Law, because it is the Law of the Infinite. We know we shall see the time when that day of sorrow which comes once a year and which by some is commemorated in sorrow throughout the year, that Friday will commemorate the glory of the Eternal Principle whose children we know we are. Thus, in growing understanding and the evolution of our own lives will we commemorate as Lightbearers our Friday of Light.

And he closed by giving the Vibrations...

Account of Lecture by Eugene Fersen
Montreal, Canada, Spring 1932

by L. Anciaux

At one of the delightful informal talks which usually take place when any of his students are gathered together, many things of great value were discussed, the following being notes upon some of the most outstanding:

Speaking in answer to a query as to the relation which Science of Being bears to religion generally, he stated emphatically that there could be no connection, because religions were built upon blind faith while Science of Being is based upon scientific investigations of natural laws; nor need there be any conflict either. Students of the Science of Being are not enemies of religions. They can well afford to ignore them and especially the attitude of certain of the clergy, who, not understanding the scope of the teaching, and being of a narrow trend of mind, oppose anything which is not orthodox. He added, there is no need to engage in useless controversy with the representatives of an institution which is already dying, attacked upon all sides by forces so powerful and so resourceful and so tremendous that there can be no doubt whatever about the outcome.

I wish you to know Fersen said, that all institutions are doomed, within a comparatively short period of time, to perish, you cannot yet perceive this, but I can, and I tell you such a change is coming. Not so much material as mental, so much that you will be amazed; it will be unbelievable, and in that change all societies, all religions, the various clubs and secret societies, welfare organizations and every organized body occupying today positions of prominence, will explode from within. You think that many changes have occurred already, but when the big upheaval comes you will remember what I am telling you. In answer to a question as to when this would occur, he stated he thought that it would be within three to four years because man could not stand more than that amount of suffering.

For this reason I have been careful not to make our organization too set, too much of an institution, and careful to keep it off a religious aspect, because I realize so clearly that nothing which is now permanent can survive. Afterwards, we can form a more suitable organization, but not before, because all is at present in a state of flux.

Speaking of the comments of some members upon the danger of symbols being regarded in a religious light, he acknowledged that there were some whose previous habits of thought and early training inclined them to regard any symbol as such, and for this reason he has reduced the symbolism to a minimum. And, after all, we must not forget that symbols are utilized by many non-religious bodies. Scientists, for instance, move and live in a world of symbols, all sorts of clubs have symbols – the Rotarians have their wheel which does not revolve, the Lions Club has a lion which does not roar – and the Lightbearers have their Light which is a living flame, a live emblem of Life.

As to the Swastika, he has already explained its meaning in various ways, but neither of these two symbols is intended to have any religious significance. As to the attitude of students towards these symbols, that was beyond his control, only growth in understanding could do this. Certain types of individuals seem to require symbolic representation more than others.

The passing of the Light at closed assemblies is the only procedure in the nature of a ceremony, which he sanctioned and it is intended to create within the mind of the recipient a sense of responsibility, first materially, because he has to hold the light when the chairman passes it to him, and then mentally, as the meaning of the light is recognized as representing the knowledge which it is his duty to pass on.

Speaking of the term Lightbearer, it is another name for Lucifer who is the Lightbearer in Mythologies, fallen it is true, because Lucifer typifies the human mind with all its errors and limitations. This name has been ground in the mire and dirt for centuries but only through the regeneration of mind can improvement come. Symbolically, that meant the uplifting of the term Lucifer as well, so for this reason, he placed the light of mind, i.e., the light used at our assemblies, on a pedestal, raised it from the mire and gave the title Lightbearers to those who are to do this great work.

The term Lightbearer will become a mark of the highest honor. Already, he said, in some centers outside of the West, the children especially were becoming very proud of being called by that name. We must be proud of it and while not allowing emotionally inclined members to emphasize or make a religion out of the sole ceremony, i.e., the passing of the light, or the symbol of the swastika, yet we should not despise those two symbols for they stand for so much.

Speaking of the future, he gave us a glimpse of the magnificent conception which he hoped would one day be a reality and told us how he had spent much money in models for the Towers of Light which he planned for each center. As he talked we saw formed by the magic of his words, lovely buildings in circular form, with a central dome within. At one end, great open sections with the blue sky, always visible, studded in stars – Nature's ceiling, heating and other arrangements to permit this in comfort.

At the other end of the Tower, like the large newspapergrams on the Times Square building, would be swiftly moving sentences formed from selected passages from the Science of Being: No preacher or minister to misinterpret them. In the center block forming a marble pedestal on which would be a bowl, the whole formed of ascending shades of marble to pure white, within which would burn lights to illuminate the marble, and the whole placed so as to stand against the blue sky of nature.

On the wall and sides, lighting effects as in a theatre would change while, maybe, a beautiful body of dancers staged a performance. Music, the best obtainable would be played. He thinks that until new geniuses arise, such music as the Song of the Volga Boatman and the Song of Flame would be appropriate for occasional playing at our assemblies.

There in the Tower of Light would be pictured graphically to us, the Lightbearers, not as to a church, but as some go to present day picture palaces, to find rest and relaxation and to commune with the Infinite; no preachers, no talk – silence over all; the silence of growing communion with our Father – scientifically explainable as an endeavor consciously and intelligently to raise ourselves in the scale of vibrations in order to reach the highest. The methods used would not be of the church, but rather a first class modern theatre where all modern scientific knowledge is brought into play in the bewilderingly beautiful panorama of lights and music, to cause within their patrons that feeling of harmony which they unconsciously seek.

So, in that pictured Tower of Light, manmade beauty would coalesce and gather inspiration from Nature's unending beauty. It must be confessed that Mr. Fersen is a master of expression for we seemed to see before us a sublimely restful idea, painted in vastly more detail than memory allows on these pages.

One seemed to see in material form the "Dream," a penned picture of the home of those heavenly twins, Love and Lucifer, that is, our dual nature, a place where Spirit of Matter is used to symbolize the identity between the two poles of nature, and as I tell it, I can hear his emphatic words, "And, such a place would be no church, nor house any religion as I conceive it."

From this he went on to outline briefly a talk which he intended to give to the students. You have now, he said, come to a stage where you have to abandon that semi-secluded attitude of letting the world go by. Lightbearers are not alone to spread the Science of Living, to meet on Fridays and to pass a light, read Science of Being and to talk aimlessly. Lightbearers are not Lightbearers unless they CARRY this Light, if they just hold the light, they are *not* Lightbearers.

For instance, there was the matter of the refusal of the jail authorities to allow Science of Being to be explained to the inmates of such institutions. Already a start had been made in persistence in following up on the matter to the end and its continuance in publishing the correspondence in our upcoming publications. Such persistence is bound to have a definite effect even if no immediate results appear.

He discussed some of his difficulties and pointed out that no matter how many disappointments he suffered, he always carried on and did not allow himself to become discouraged. You may not realize it, he offered, but I am fighting a battle and its front extends to both planes, visible and invisible. I trace its effect in subtle disintegration, in fear and mistrust accorded me so often by utter strangers; in all manner of obstacles to my work. These are all subtle evidences of the battle raging about which you know little or nothing, and which I am carrying on single handed, but undiscouraged. I know I have Right on my side and Right must eventually win. You see, a partial picture, I see more of it, that is all, and though I was left all alone to carry on the battle, I should still continue to teach my fellow beings that which alone can lead them to sanity.

Do you know, he said, that every one of us is unbalanced, disharmonious, that is, insane? And do you know that from my study of people in asylums, I have found that those more violently insane people have the peculiarity that they imagine the sane ones around them to be insane. The same is with the others outside asylums: everyone is insane, and when one not quite so insane gets up to tell them the truth, they think him or her insane. It is a terrible condition, which some day I shall succeed in overcoming. But do not think that I am ever discouraged.

Speaking of Science Of Being, he reminded us that we must never regard it as a religion or a new cult or an ism of any kind. It is far more than that, for it embraces a study of Life itself.

I have plans for our organization, which contemplate it as the foundation of enlightenment, the ladder towards a realm of good government based upon the Four Square Principle, known as the Great Law. That this will, with the help of The Great Law, be a fact; you can be assured.

THE END
Written by L. Anciaux

Thus ended a memorable address, so simply delivered that I could not feel even the expected resistance of those strangers whose religious concepts were thus laid bare in all their crude nakedness as illustrations. And, all this by one whose remembrance of the events which transpired twenty centuries ago are as clear as the day they happened. How few will believe the amazing truth. They cannot realize that the greatest character of all time stands once more giving words of Truth, telling of things which if listened to would change the face of the world. The greatest tragedy of all is not that the so called evil doers will not listen, but that those who consider themselves the acme of spirituality, the depositories of knowledge, the sustainers of good, it is they who have been tried in the balance and been found wanting. Verily, was it said, "Not all those who cry Lord, Lord, shall enter into the kingdom of Light."

But, no matter, there are those who have surmounted veritable mountains of prejudice and ignorance and who have emerged into the clear atmosphere of understanding. They do not condemn, for of all the amazing things this is the most amazing and they well realize the difficulties they themselves had to overcome in order to rise to the heights of pure knowledge offered them. Those comparatively few will remain, no matter what happens, as witnesses of Truth, ready at the proper moment to throw their full force in the scale of all that is and cannot be taken from them as long as they understand and follow the Law, wherever it should lead them. They are a great company, crusaders of the twentieth century with a mission as noble as any in history and with the help of the Great Law and the inspiring example of their leader, they will not be found wanting.

Original Public Lecture Announcements
of
Eugene Fersen, L.

THE LIGHTBEARERS
of Washington, D. C.

Announce their Leader

EUGENE FERSEN, L.
Originator and Teacher of the Science of Being

in

Three Important Free Public Lectures

ON MAN'S LATENT POWERS AND HOW TO DEVELOP THEM

Subjects:

Sunday, January 24th, at 8:15 P. M.
   WHATS WRONG WITH US TODAY.

Monday, January 25th, at 8:15 P. M.
   THE PRISON AND YOU THE PRISONER.

Tuesday, January 26th, at 8:15 P. M.
   WIN OR LOSE -- THE DIFFERENCE BETWEEN.

In the Ballroom of the
HOTEL ARLINGTON
1025 Vermont Avenue N. W.

All Welcome   Washington, D. C.   Collection
                            1932

March 3rd – 14th 1925   4

"KNOW THYSELF AND THOU SHALT KNOW ALL"

*Three Inspiring Free
Public Lectures*

on

Man's Latent Powers and How to Develop Them

Tuesday　　March 3rd—"THROUGH MATTER TO SPIRIT"

Wednesday　March 4th—"LOST POWERS REDEEMED"

Thursday　　March 5th—"CREATIVE THOUGHT"

By

EUGENE FERSEN

President of THE LIGHTBEARERS
An International Educational, Scientific and Humanitarian Organization
Originator and Teacher of Science of Being

AT 8:15 P. M.

WOMANS CLUB AUDITORIUM
1320 South Fourth Avenue, Louisville, Ky.

All Welcome　　　　　　　　　　　　　　　　　Collection

Baron Eugene Fersen

of Moscow, Russia

METAPHYSICAL TEACHER and HEALER

will give an important lecture on

"Man's Latent Forces and How to Use Them"

8 P. M. SUNDAY, MAY 9

Lecture Hall, Carnegie Institute, Forbes Street

INVITE YOUR　　　　　　　　　　ADMISSION
FRIENDS　　　　　　　　　　　　FREE

FREE PUBLIC LECTURE

on

𝕮𝖍𝖊 𝕾𝖈𝖎𝖊𝖓𝖈𝖊 𝖔𝖋 𝕹𝖚𝖒𝖇𝖊𝖗𝖘

by

EUGENE FERSEN, L.

Leader of THE LIGHTBEARERS

A Humanitarian, Educational Organization

Based on Laws of Nature, explaining the innermost secrets of Life itself, esoteric and at the same time exoteric also, entirely different from all the various known theories on Ancient and Modern Numerology, the Science of Numbers as revealed by Eugene Fersen, is a unique and most outstanding contribution to Practical and Occult Knowledge in the Science of Life.

PRINTED IN U.S.A.

卐

"KNOW THYSELF AND THOU SHALT KNOW ALL"

FAREWELL ENGAGEMENT

FOUR FREE PUBLIC LECTURES

ON

SCIENCE OF BEING

BY

EUGENE FERSEN
(SVETOZAR)

International President of THE LIGHTBEARERS

AND

Originator of the Science of Being

THE TEACHINGS THAT WILL SHOW YOU HOW TO GET THE MOST AND BEST OUT OF LIFE BY USING CERTAIN LAWS AND FORCES OF THE UNIVERSE TO DEVELOP YOUR OWN LATENT POWERS OF BODY, MIND AND SOUL.

Subjects:

SUNDAY, MARCH 13TH, 3:00 P.M.—GOD AND SCIENCE.
SUNDAY, MARCH 13TH, 8:15 P.M.—HOW TO TAP THE SOURCE OF ALL POWER.
MONDAY, MARCH 14TH, 8:15 P.M.—REJUVENATION.
TUESDAY, MARCH 15TH, 8:15 P.M.—MAKING LIFE PAY.

1927

These Lectures will be followed by courses in "Science of Being" (See Pages 2 and 3)

BALLROOM

PALLISER HOTEL   CALGARY, ALTA.

PUBLIC CORDIALLY WELCOMED   SILVER COLLECTION

"KNOW THYSELF AND THOU SHALT KNOW ALL."

FIVE
Free Public Lectures
ON
Science of Being
BY
EUGENE FERSEN
[SVETOZAR]

President of THE LIGHTBEARERS
AND
Originator of the Science of Being

THE TEACHINGS THAT WILL SHOW YOU HOW TO GET THE MOST AND BEST OUT OF LIFE BY USING CERTAIN LAWS AND FORCES OF THE UNIVERSE TO DEVELOP YOUR OWN LATENT POWERS OF BODY, MIND AND SOUL.

Sunday,   May 15th, 3:00 P. M.—THE SLEEPING GIANT WITHIN YOU.
Sunday,   May 15th, 8:15 P. M.—THE FINE ART OF LIVING.
Monday,   May 16th, 8:15 P. M.—HOW TO TAP THE SOURCE OF ALL POWER.
Tuesday,   May 17th, 8:15 P. M.—SHORT CUTS TO SUCCESS.
Wednesday, May 18th, 8:15 P. M.—MAKING LIFE PAY.

1927

These Lectures will be followed by courses in "Science of Being" (See Pages 2 and 3)

BALLROOM
HOTEL UTAH   SALT LAKE CITY, UTAH

PUBLIC CORDIALLY WELCOMED   *SILVER OFFERING*

BARON EUGENE FERSEN, L.

OF MOSCOW, RUSSIA

President of the LightBearers
An International Scientific and Educational Organization

Will Deliver Two Free Public Lectures

———ON———

"Man's Latent Forces and How to Develop Them"

Tuesday, March 7th, . . 8:15 P. M.
Wednesday, March 8th, 8:15 P. M.

EMERY AUDITORIUM

CANAL AND WALNUT STREETS

CINCINNATI, OHIO

To be followed by Two Courses of Special Class Instructions.

For Particulars and Dates see next Page.

ADMISSION FREE! COLLECTION!

(Copyrighted)

BARON EUGENE FERSEN

Originator and Teacher
OF THE

TRIUNE SYSTEM

Will give two free Lectures

"THE GREATEST INVESTMENT"

IN TWO PARTS

Tuesday, Nov. 15th   Wednesday, Nov. 16th

At 8 p. m.

Elks Temple

Gass Ave., and Lafayette Blvd.,
DETROIT, MICH.

The Lecture will be followed by a Course of Seven Lessons in the Practical

SCIENCE OF BEING

(TRIUNE SYSTEM)

Starting Friday, November 18th, at 8 p. m.

AT

THE TWENTIETH CENTURY CLUB

62 E. Columbia Street

For further information apply to

Mr. P. A. Hathaway or Mr. V. E. Vladikin

Hotel Tuller

Admission Free.   Bring Your Friends.   Collection

Baron Eugene Fersen

of Moscow, Russia

Nephew of the late Count Tolstoi

ORIGINATOR AND TEACHER
OF THE

Triune Harmonial System

Scientifically based on the Law of Vibration

will train a private class in both the scientific principles and the personal demonstration of the Triune Harmonial System, which will explain the laws under which the Universal Forces of Nature operate and their application to the problems of every-day life so to bring into complete harmony the body, mind and Soul, also physical conditions and environment.

The Triune Harmonial System (body, mind and Soul) teaches the adjustment, not only of the individual to his own harmonious status, but also of individuals to others, and in general the transformation of everything into an harmonious whole, thus bringing harmony out of all the inharmonies and limitations in life—poverty, ill-health, lack of poise, lack of concentration, mental inefficiency, etc.

The private class consisting of seven lesson-demonstrations will be held as follows:

Monday, Nov. 29.   Saturday, Dec. 4.
Tuesday, Nov. 30.   Tuesday, December 7.
Thursday, Dec. 2.   Thursday, Dec. 9.
         Saturday, Dec. 11.
              at 8 p. m.

At GREEN HOTEL
South Raymond Ave., Pasadena

For further information apply to
MRS. FLORENCE B. CURTISS
480 Lincoln Ave., Pasadena
Phone Colo. 1868

TICKETS

FOR A

COURSE OF SEVEN CLASS LESSONS

(Personal Training and Demonstration)

GIVEN BY

BARON EUGENE FERSEN

ORIGINATOR AND TEACHER OF

THE TRIUNE HARMONIAL SYSTEM

STARTING FRIDAY, FEBRUARY 11th, at 8 P.M.

BLUE ROOM VANCOUVER HOTEL

On Sale at
Mr HARRY McINTOSH
114 CROWN BUILDING   Phone Seymour ~~2225~~ 2221

Mr. D. D. ENGLAND
204 NICOLA STREET   Phone R. F. 1542-R

TERMS: FULL COURSE OF TRAINING FIFTY DOLLARS
PAYMENTS BY INSTALLMENTS
NO ADMISSION FOR SINGLE LESSON

IN ORDER TO SIMPLIFY REGISTRATION, KINDLY DO SO
IN ADVANCE

[Stamp: Corrected address to O'Brien Hall Hastings St. W.]

Baron Eugene Fersen
OF MOSCOW, RUSSIA
Originator and Teacher
of the
TRIUNE HARMONIAL SYSTEM
Scientifically based on the Law of Vibration

WILL GIVE TWO IMPORTANT FREE LECTURES

MONDAY, FEBRUARY 7th
AT 8 P. M.

"THE GREAT CALL"

TUESDAY, FEBRUARY 8th
AT 8 P. M.

"HEALING THROUGH LAWS AND FORCES OF NATURE"

At the
MASONIC TEMPLE
Harvard and Pine Streets
SEATTLE, WASHINGTON

—o—

The Lectures will be followed by a Course of Seven Lessons
in the practical

SCIENCE OF BEING
(Triune Harmonial System)
FINE ARTS HALL
Fourth Avenue, between Seneca and University St.

—o—

For further information apply to:
MRS. MARIE JENSEN PARK
HOTEL LEE,
SEATTLE, WASHINGTON

—o—

Bring your Friends   *Admission Free*   *Collection*

Baron Eugene Fersen, L.B.L.

Will deliver two important lectures

— ON —

"Healing Powers"

Wednesday, Jan. 11th—
"Mind Force"

Thursday, Jan. 12th—
"Life Energy"

AT 8:15 P. M.

ST. JOHN'S CATHEDRAL
AUDITORIUM

500 JACKSON STREET
MILWAUKEE

Admission Free   Collection

Baron Eugene Fersen, L. B.

Metaphysical Teacher and Healer

Will deliver two important lectures

—— ON ——

"The Healing of the Future"

Tuesday, Dec. 13th—"Life Energy"

**Wednesday, Dec. 14th—
"Mind Force and Spiritual Power"**

AT 8:15 P. M.

PALM ROOM
THE ST. PAUL HOTEL
ST. PAUL, MINN.

Admission Free   Collection

Baron Eugene Fersen
of Moscow, Russia
Nephew of the late Count Tolstoi

ORIGINATOR AND TEACHER
OF THE

Triune Harmonial System
Scientifically based on the Law of Vibration

will train a private class in both the scientific principles and the personal demonstration of the Triune Harmonial System, which will explain the laws under which the Universal Forces of Nature operate and their application to the problems of every-day life so to bring into complete harmony the body, mind and Soul, also physical conditions and environment.

The Triune Harmonial System (body, mind and Soul) teaches the adjustment, not only of the individual to his own harmonious status, but also of individuals to others, and in general the transformation of everything into an harmonious whole, thus bringing harmony out of all the inharmonies and limitations in life—poverty, ill-health, lack of poise, lack of concentration, mental inefficiency, etc.

Seven lesson-demonstrations as follows:

Wednesday, Nov. 24.	Wednesday, Dec. 1.
Friday, Nov. 26.	Friday, Dec. 3.
Saturday, Nov. 27.	Monday, Dec. 6.

Wednesday Dec. 8.

At SYMPHONY HALL
Blanchard Building
Hill Street entrance.   Los Angeles

For further information apply to Mr. MAX AEPPLI
Hotel Stowell, Los Angeles
Phone Main 5776

PROSPERITY IS POWER!

Why not be prosperous?

- EVERYBODY CAN LEARN IT -

Eugene Fersen, L.
WILL EXPLAIN IT.

—⊗—

Like every other form of dis-harmony — lack of Prosperity, which expresses itself thru Material, Mental and Spiritual Limitations, is a condition of **dis-ease,** which should be and can be cured.

The following Course of Six Lessons of practical instruction **of how to demonstrate in one's own life ABUNDANCE,** in spite even of adverse conditions, is the result of the author's many years of investigations thruout the world of Conditions and Causes of unemployment, failures and want. This Course will give to the students a satisfactory, practical solution of a problem; which to the majority of human beings is of such a vital importance.

Baron Eugene Fersen, L. B.

Metaphysical Teacher and Healer

Will deliver two important lectures

—— ON ——

"The Healing of the Future"

Thursday, Dec. 8th—"Life Energy"

Friday, Dec. 9th—
"Mind Force and Spiritual Power"

AT 8:15 P. M.

UNITARIAN CHURCH

8th Street and La Salle Avenue

MINNEAPOLIS, MINN.

Admission Free   Collection

BARON EUGENE FERSEN, L.

OF MOSCOW, RUSSIA

President of the LightBearers
An International Scientific and Educational Organization

Will Deliver Two Free Public Lectures

ON

"Man's Latent Powers and How to Develop Them"

SUNDAY, APRIL 2nd............8:15 P. M.
MONDAY, APRIL 3rd............8:15 P. M.

Ball Room, New Willard Hotel
Washington, D. C.

For further information apply to
Mr. J. A. Guintyllo and Mr. P. A. Hathaway
At the Hotel Bellevue, McPherson Square. Phone, Main 800
For Particulars and Dates See Next Page

ADMISSION FREE!   COLLECTION!

Baron Eugene Fersen

OF MOSCOW, RUSSIA
Originator and Teacher
of the

TRIUNE HARMONIAL SYSTEM

Scientifically based on the Law of Vibration

WILL GIVE TWO IMPORTANT FREE LECTURES

MONDAY, FEBRUARY 28th, 8 p. m.

"THE DAWN OF THE DAY OF FREEDOM"

—o—

TUESDAY, MARCH 1st, 8 p. m.

"HEALING THROUGH LAWS AND FORCES OF NATURE"

At the

AUDITORIUM OF THE PYTHIAN BUILDING

388 YAMHILL ST.

The Lectures will be followed by a Course of Seven Lessons
in the practical

SCIENCE OF BEING

(Triune Harmonial System)

MULTNOMAH HOTEL, PORTLAND, OREGON

—o—

For further information apply to:
MRS. L. F. MacGREGOR
413-433 CHAMBER OF COMMERCE BLDG.

—o—

MR. V. E. VLADIKIN, Secretary
MULTNOMAH HOTEL, PORTLAND, OREGON

Bring your Friends   *Admission Free*   *Collection*

Baron Eugene Fersen
OF MOSCOW, RUSSIA

METAPHYSICAL TEACHER *and* HEALER

WILL GIVE THE FOLLOWING LECTURES AT

Blanchard Hall
233 South Broadway, Los Angeles

Wednesday November 17th, 8 p. m.
"THE DAWN OF A NEW DAY"

Thursday, November 18th, 8 p. m.
"MAN'S LATENT FORCES and
HOW TO USE THEM"

Friday, November 19th, 8 p. m.
"THE HEALING OF THE FUTURE"

Shakespeare Hall
220 South Los Robles Street
PASADENA

Monday, November 22nd, 8. p. m.
"THE HEALING OF THE FUTURE"

Invite your friends :: *Admission free* :: *Collection*

Baron Eugene Fersen, L.B.L.

Will deliver two important lectures

— ON —

"Healing Powers"

Monday, January 9th—
"Mind Force"

Tuesday, January 10th—
"Life Energy"

AT 8:15 P. M.

ORCHESTRA HALL

220 South Michigan Boulevard

CHICAGO

Admission Free   Collection

Baron Eugene Fersen

OF MOSCOW, RUSSIA
Originator and Teacher
of the

TRIUNE HARMONIAL SYSTEM

Scientifically based on the Law of Vibration

WILL GIVE TWO IMPORTANT FREE LECTURES

SUNDAY, FEBRUARY 6

At 3 P. M.

"THE DAWN OF A NEW DAY"

At 8 P. M.

'THE HEALING OF THE FUTURE'

DOMINION THEATRE, VANCOUVER, B. C.

The Lectures will be followed by a Course of Seven Lessons
in the practical

SCIENCE OF BEING

(Triune Harmonial System)

BLUE ROOM, VANCOUVER HOTEL

—o—

For further information apply to:

Mr. HARRY McINTOSH

114 CROWN BUILDING   Phone Seymour 2225

—o—

Mr. D. D. ENGLAND

204 NICOLA STREET   Phone R. F. 1542-R

—o—

Bring your Friends   *Admission Free*   *Collection*

Corrected address for classes: O'Brien Hall, Hastings St. W.

Baron

Eugene Fersen

OF MOSCOW, RUSSIA

Originator and Teacher

OF THE

TRIUNE SYSTEM

Scientifically based on the Law of Vibration

WILL GIVE TWO IMPORTANT FREE LECTURES

WEDNESDAY, OCTOBER 19th
at 8 P.M.

"Forces and Powers Latent in Man and How to Use Them"

THURSDAY, OCTOBER 20th
at 8 P.M.

"The Healing of the Future"

AT THE

CITY CONVENTION HALL
Washington Sq.
Rochester, N. Y.

The Lectures will be followed by a Course of Seven Lessons in the practical

SCIENCE OF BEING
(TRIUNE SYSTEM)

Starting Monday, October 24th, at 8 P.M.

AT

CULVER HALL
708 University Ave.

For further information apply to:

MR. V. E. VLADIKIN

THE POWERS HOTEL : ROCHESTER, N. Y.

Bring Your Friends   Admission Free   Collection

Baron Eugene Fersen

OF MOSCOW, RUSSIA

Originator and Teacher

of the

TRIUNE HARMONIAL SYSTEM

Will train in March in Denver a Private Class of Seven Lessons in both the scientific principles and the personal Demonstration of his **TRIUNE HARMONIAL SYSTEM**, which explains the laws under which the Universal Forces of Nature operate and their application to the problems of everyday life, so as to bring into complete harmony the body, the mind, and the Soul, also physical conditions and environment.

This will not involve any modification of one's religious beliefs, but a purely scientific demonstration, not merely theoretical lectures, but each student is taught to **demonstrate his powers** during the class.

For further information and for tickets apply to:

MRS. N. ANDERSON

1136 BANNOCK STREET   Phone No. Main 5511

DENVER (COLORADO)

Baron Eugene Fersen

OF MOSCOW, RUSSIA

Originator and Teacher

of the

TRIUNE HARMONIAL SYSTEM

Scientifically based on the Law of Vibration

WILL GIVE TWO IMPORTANT FREE LECTURES

THURSDAY, APRIL 21st
At 8 P. M.

"THE DAWN OF THE DAY OF FREEDOM"

---o---

FRIDAY, APRIL 22nd
At 3 P. M.   At 8 P. M.

"HEALING OF OTHERS AND ONESELF THROUGH LAWS AND FORCES OF NATURE"

At the

AUDITORIUM OF THE MEMORIAL HALL
PITTSBURGH, PA.

The Lectures will be followed by a Course of Seven Lessons in the practical

SCIENCE OF BEING
(Triune Harmonial System)

BANQUET HALL of the MEMORIAL HALL
FIFTH AVE. AND GRANT BOULEVARD

---o---

For further information apply to:

MISS ESSIE GILLIAN SCHENCK

233 OLIVER AVENUE

PITTSBURGH, PA.   Phone Grant 2522 R

Bring your Friends   Admission Free   Collection

Baron Eugene Fersen

OF MOSCOW, RUSSIA
Originator and Teacher
of the

TRIUNE HARMONIAL SYSTEM

Scientifically based on the Law of Vibration
WILL GIVE TWO IMPORTANT FREE LECTURES

MONDAY, APRIL 4th
At 8 P. M.

"THE POWER THAT LIBERATES"

—o—

TUESDAY, APRIL 5th
AT 8 P. M.

"HEALING OTHERS AND ONESELF THROUGH LAWS AND FORCES OF NATURE"

At the

SCOTTISH RITE BUILDING
(Southwest Corner) Broad and Race Streets
PHILADELPHIA, PA.

The Lectures will be followed by a Course of Seven Lessons
in the practical

SCIENCE OF BEING
(Triune Harmonial System)

MUSICAL ART CLUB HALL
1811 RAUSTEAD STREET

—o—

For further information apply to:
MISS EDNA SLEEPER
1803 Chestnut Street, Philadelphia
Phone Locust 6945

Bring your Friends   *Admission Free*   *Collection*

Baron Eugene Fersen

OF MOSCOW, RUSSIA

METAPHYSICAL TEACHER and HEALER

WILL GIVE THREE IMPORTANT LECTURES ON

SUNDAY, OCTOBER 24th

3 P. M.   The Dawn of a New Day.

8 P. M.   Man's Latent Forces and How to Use Them.

SCOTTISH RITE LECTURE HALL
1290 SUTTER STREET

WEDNESDAY, OCTOBER 27th,
8 P. M.

The Healing of the Future

SCOTTISH RITE AUDITORIUM
VAN NESS AVE. AND SUTTER ST.

Introduced by Dr. F. Homer Curtiss of New York

INVITE YOUR FRIENDS :: ADMISSION FREE :: COLLECTION

PROSPERITY IS POWER!!!

Why not be prosperous?

- EVERYBODY CAN LEARN IT -

EUGENE FERSEN, L,
Will Explain It.

1911

❧

Like every other form of dis-harmony—lack of Prosperity, which expresses itself thru Material, Mental and Spiritual Limitations, is a condition of **dis-ease,** which should be and can be cured.

The following Course of Six Lessons of practical instruction **of how to demonstrate in one's own life ABUNDANCE,** inspite even of adverse conditions, is the result of the author's many years of investigations thruout the world of Conditions and Causes of unemployment, failures and want. This Course will give to the students a satisfactory, practical solution of a problem, which to the majority of human beings is of such a vital importance.

SCIENCE OF BEING
(The Science of Constructive Living)

BY

EUGENE FERSEN, L.

Advanced Course

The Seven Fundamental Laws
Governing Everything in Nature, including Man

Baron Eugene Fersen

OF MOSCOW, RUSSIA

Originator and Teacher

of the

TRIUNE HARMONIAL SYSTEM

Scientifically based on the Law of Vibration

WILL GIVE TWO IMPORTANT FREE LECTURES

MONDAY, FEBRUARY 7th

AT 8 P. M.

"THE GREAT CALL"

TUESDAY, FEBRUARY 8th

AT 8 P. M.

"HEALING THROUGH LAWS AND FORCES OF NATURE"

At the

MASONIC TEMPLE

Harvard and Pine Streets

SEATTLE, WASHINGTON

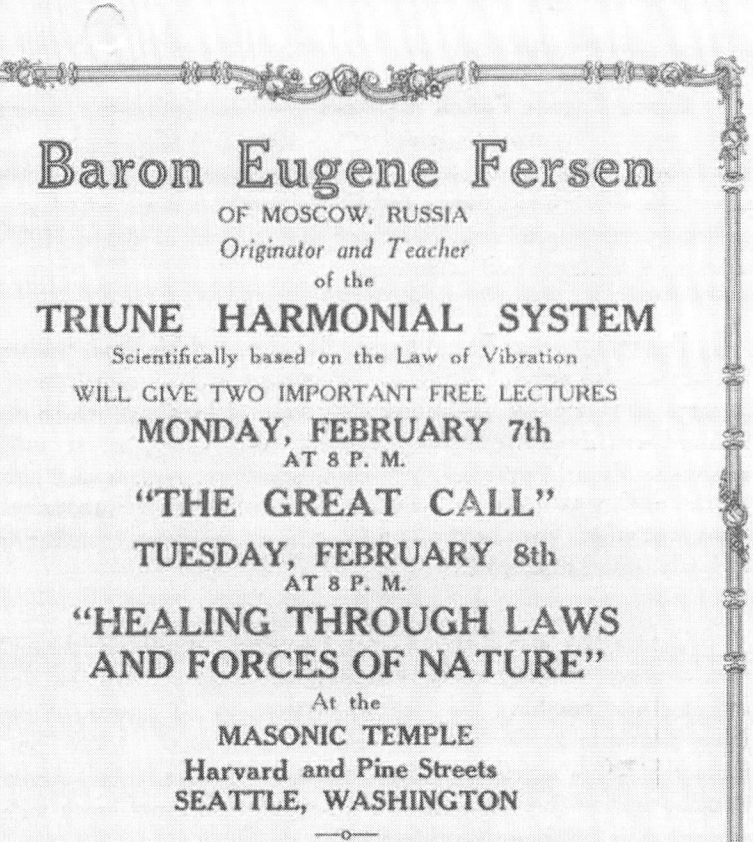

---o---

The Lectures will be followed by a Course of Seven Lessons in the practical

SCIENCE OF BEING

(Triune Harmonial System)

FINE ARTS HALL

Fourth Avenue, between Seneca and University St.

---o---

For further information apply to:

MRS. MARIE JENSEN PARK

HOTEL LEE,

SEATTLE, WASHINGTON

---o---

Bring your Friends   *Admission Free*   *Collection*

THE LIGHTBEARERS JUNIOR CLASSES

Held Once Each Week
from
September First to June First

Classroom
Suite 107, Securities Building
1904 Third Avenue
Phone SEneca 9356

"KNOW THYSELF AND THOU SHALT KNOW ALL"

YOUR CHILD'S OPPORTUNITY

THE LIGHTBEARERS offer to YOUR CHILD the opportunity to get the right start in Life, by teaching him THE SCIENCE OF BEING! It is an opportunity to get a Training and Knowledge, at an early age, that will be of TREMENDOUS VALUE to him at all times!

THE SCIENCE OF BEING, originated by Eugene Fersen, L., explains the Fundamental Principles of Existence. It is presented in a simple, direct manner by the Educational Secretaries, in classes divided as to age. Any boy or girl, between four and twenty-one years of age, and who has the consent of his parents, is eligible to attend. The only charge connected with this work is a small voluntary offering on the part of the children, which is used to help meet the expenses involved.

In these Classes, the children are taught THE SCIENCE OF BEING at an age when they are most able to assimilate this Knowledge, and use it to great advantage. The parents of children who have had this Training, invariably report marked results in their development. It is especially noticeable in the improvement in their school work, many having risen from mediocre to good, and sometimes brilliant students!

THE SCIENCE OF BEING accomplishes Its results through the development of a child's TRUE CHARACTER and SELF-RELIANCE. It teaches him how to meet his problems; how to overcome ALL kinds of bad characteristics, such as laziness, timidity, rudeness, lack of self-control, lethargy, and even sickness!

THE SCIENCE OF BEING teaches a child how to build a Strong and Healthy Body. It develops his Mind, giving him the capacity to learn easily and think clearly. Through It, he learns the lesson of Proper and Constructive Conduct, thus making him Truthful and Law-abiding, and willing to cooperate with his parents. One of the most important things he gains is the ability to get along with others, and to be liked by everyone with whom he comes in contact. Above all, he is given an Understanding of his Purpose in Life, and with it, a Confidence in himself and his Ability to Succeed in all he undertakes.

"*Know Thyself and Thou Shalt Know All*"

BARON EUGENE FERSEN
OF MOSCOW, RUSSIA

President of
LIGHTBEARERS
An International Scientific and Educational Organization

WILL DELIVER TWO FREE PUBLIC LECTURES ON

"Man's Latent Powers and How to Develop Them"

Thursday, March 1st, "The Master Mind"
Friday, March 2nd, "The Greatest Power"

AT 8:15 P. M.

Convention Hall
HOTEL HENRY WATTERSON
Walnut Street, between 4th and 5th Sts.
Louisville, Ky.

For further information apply to
MISS ARDATH BROWNELL
Hotel Henry Watterson

Admission Free — Collection

These lectures to be followed by two courses of
Special Instruction in "Science of Being"

Public Healings

by

EUGENE FERSEN, L.

Leader of THE LIGHTBEARERS

*

EVERY SUNDAY at 8:15 p.m. sharp

The MASONIC TEMPLE
PORTLAND, OREGON

Of Nature's inexhaustible Forces and Powers, one Power is the most important of all, as It is the Foundation of Life Itself, and that is "THE ENERGY OF THE UNIVERSE," which, in a certain aspect, is known today to Scientists under the name of the Magnetic Current of Nature. This Power, contacted, by a special method, discovered by Eugene Fersen, originator of "The Science of Being" and founder and leader of THE LIGHTBEARERS, is used in the Public Healing Assemblies which every Sunday Eugene Fersen is holding in Portland for the benefit of all who are afflicted with ailments, physical, mental and emotional.

PRINTED IN THE U.S.A.

BARON EUGENE FERSEN, L.

OF MOSCOW, RUSSIA

President of the LightBearers
An International Scientific and Educational Organization

Will Deliver Two Free Public Lectures

———ON———

"Man's Latent Forces and How to Develop Them"

Tuesday, March 7th, . . 8:15 P. M.
Wednesday, March 8th, 8:15 P. M.

EMERY AUDITORIUM

CANAL AND WALNUT STREETS

CINCINNATI, OHIO

To be followed by Two Courses of Special Class Instructions.

For Particulars and Dates see next Page.

ADMISSION FREE!　　　　　　　　COLLECTION!

(Copyrighted)

BARON EUGENE FERSEN, L.

OF MOSCOW, RUSSIA

President of the LightBearers
An International Scientific and Educational Organization

Will Deliver Two Free Public Lectures

ON

"Man's Latent Powers and How to Develop Them"

Monday, April 17th, 8:15 P. M.

Tuesday, April 18th, 8:15 P. M.

Ball Room Hotel Powers
Rochester

For further information apply to
Mr. J. A. Guintyllo and Mr. P. A. Hathaway at the Hotel Powers
Phone, Stone 4500
For Particulars and Dates See Next Page

ADMISSION FREE!   COLLECTION!

Public Lecture

by

EUGENE FERSEN, L.

on

"The Inner Powers of Mind"

at

Nobody can live a happy, successful life without knowing what prevents one to live such a life. The following course on the "Inner Powers of Mind" explains those Mental Powers and teaches how to use them to overcome anything that interferes with Human Progress and Happiness.

ADMISSION FREE　　　　　　　　**ALL WELCOME**

FREE ILLUSTRATED PUBLIC LECTURE

by

EUGENE FERSEN, L.

Originator and Teacher of

"THE SCIENCE OF BEING"

(The Art of Living)

Subconsciousness Photographed

Tuesday, September 17 at 8:15 P.M.

at

THE GOLD ROOM
Hotel Roosevelt, Seattle, Wash.

Mind and its Subconsciousness is Man's greatest Power for Good and Evil. A Trained Mind is the builder of an adventurous, interesting, healthy, constructive, well-balanced, successful and happy life.—Untrained, without knowledge of its own subconsciousness and lacking Self-Discipline, it becomes a destructive weapon in the hands of those who wield it, sowing disappointments, boredom, physical and mental sickness, misery, failure and unhappiness. To each human being is given the freedom to make the choice, which will then infallibly determine the future of their life,—to win or lose! ! ! What will be that choice?

PRINTED IN U.S.A.

PROSPERITY IS POWER!

Why not be prosperous?

- EVERYBODY CAN LEARN IT -

Eugene Fersen, L.
WILL EXPLAIN IT.

Like every other form of dis-harmony — lack of Prosperity, which expresses itself thru Material, Mental and Spiritual Limitations, is a condition of **dis-ease,** which should be and can be cured.

The following Course of Six Lessons of practical instruction **of how to demonstrate in one's own life ABUNDANCE,** in spite even of adverse conditions, is the result of the author's many years of investigations thruout the world of Conditions and Causes of unemployment, failures and want. This Course will give to the students a satisfactory, practical solution of a problem, which to the majority of human beings is of such a vital importance.

BARON EUGENE FERSEN

OF MOSCOW, RUSSIA

Nephew of the late Count Leo Tolstoi

ORIGINATOR AND TEACHER

OF THE

Triune Harmonial System

Scientifically based on the Law of Vibration

WILL GIVE A LECTURE AT

The U. S. Grant Hotel

326 Broadway, San Diego, California

Tuesday, December 7th at 8 p. m.

"THE HEALING OF THE FUTURE"

Invite your friends : Admission free : Collection

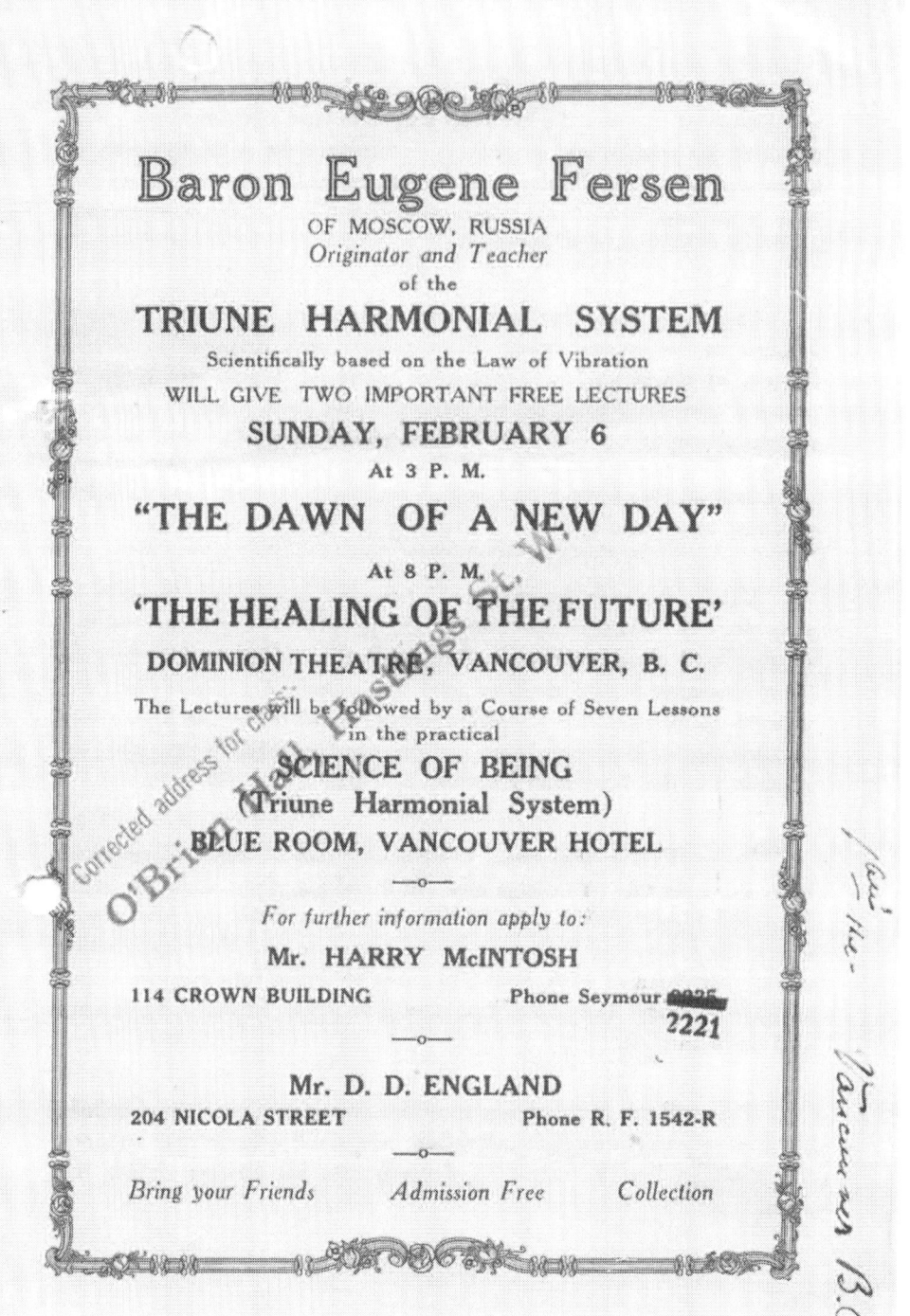

Baron Eugene Fersen

OF MOSCOW, RUSSIA

Originator and Teacher

of the

TRIUNE HARMONIAL SYSTEM

Scientifically based on the Law of Vibration

WILL GIVE TWO IMPORTANT FREE LECTURES

SUNDAY, FEBRUARY 6

At 3 P. M.

"THE DAWN OF A NEW DAY"

At 8 P. M.

'THE HEALING OF THE FUTURE'

DOMINION THEATRE, VANCOUVER, B. C.

The Lectures will be followed by a Course of Seven Lessons
in the practical

SCIENCE OF BEING

(Triune Harmonial System)

BLUE ROOM, VANCOUVER HOTEL

For further information apply to:

Mr. HARRY McINTOSH

114 CROWN BUILDING　　　Phone Seymour 2221

Mr. D. D. ENGLAND

204 NICOLA STREET　　　Phone R. F. 1542-R

Bring your Friends　　Admission Free　　Collection

[handwritten: Corrected address for classes Hall Hastings St. W., O'Brien]

BARON EUGENE FERSEN

Originator and Teacher

OF THE

TRIUNE SYSTEM

Will give two free Lectures

"THE KEY TO POWER"

IN TWO PARTS

Wednesday, Nov. 9th   Thursday, Nov. 10th

At 8 p. m.

Hotel Winton
CLEVELAND

The Lecture will be followed by a Course of Seven Lessons in the Practical

SCIENCE OF BEING
(TRIUNE SYSTEM)

Starting Monday, November 14th, at 8 p. m.

AT

HOTEL WINTON

For further information apply to

Mr. P. A. Hathaway or Mr. V. E. Vladikin

Hotel Winton, Phone, Prospect 3380

Admission Free.   Bring Your Friends.   Collection

Baron Eugene Fersen, L.B.L.

Will deliver two important lectures

— ON —

"Healing Powers"

Wednesday, Jan. 11th—
"Mind Force"

Thursday, Jan. 12th—
"Life Energy"

AT 8:15 P. M.

ST. JOHN'S CATHEDRAL
AUDITORIUM

500 JACKSON STREET
MILWAUKEE

Admission Free   Collection

FREE PUBLIC LECTURE

by

EUGENE FERSEN, L.

on

REINCARNATION

(Do the Dead Come Back to Live Again?)

Since thousands of years Reincarnation has been taught and accepted with excellent results by over a billion people of the East, yet it is hardly known by the western world. Many strange things amongst them the seeming injustices of Life, like poverty, sickness, hard luck, disharmony are explained by the Law of Reincarnation. Eugene Fersen, originator of "The Science of Being," gives a scientific explanation of why Reincarnation is a basic principle, the Law of Life, on Earth; a Law which everybody should know, because it reveals the secrets of the countless "Why's" in everybody's life.

PRINTED IN THE U.S.A.

Section IV:

Science Of Being ~ Lightbearers Art & Information

"Eyes are the 'Windows of the Mind,' not the Soul."

~ Eugene Fersen

Information for the Reader

(The following information was a packaging insert describing the creation of the original text of the leather bound special edition of Science Of Being 7 Lessons.)

The book, "Science of Being," by Eugene Fersen, has been written according to the principles contained therein. While dictating the lessons, the author contacted Universal Life Energy each time before starting the dictation. Thus, this power is actually embodied in every sentence. In other words, from the very beginning the contact between the material book and Universal Life Energy was established, making the book an actual magnetic center for the concentration of that Force. Since the fundamental principles of the teachings aim toward the Highest, appropriate physical channels had to be established for the Universal Power to flow through. The unity of the teachings had to be expressed through material unity also.

Gold, which represents the pure Mental Ray, was taken as the basis for the color scheme of the book. In its most condensed shade of dark brown, it is used in the binding and in the general print of the book. In its golden shade it is used to emphasize important sentences. The glittering golden print produces a very deep impression on the subconsciousness of the reader, acting as a luminous sign. The ivory tint of the paper is another shade of gold, in its faintest aspect. This color scheme is restful and pleasing to the eye and is a striking example of how the Law of Polarity, prevailing in most books, which are printed on white paper with black ink, can be successfully overcome.

The paper used in this book is of Ivory color India Bible. This is the first time in the history of paper manufacturing in the United States that such a paper has been made. Though extremely light and thin, the paper is of the highest grade and possesses great wearing qualities, making a book for practical daily use.

A special type, very legible and at the same time beautiful and original was selected.

Malcolm Thurburn, well-known English artist, was commissioned to make the lettering, ornamentation and the illustrations for the title pages, which are individual for each lesson.

The emblem of the Science of Being is stamped in pure gold on the cover, and all materials used in the making of the book are of the highest obtainable quality, this being essentially important, not only from the artistic point of view, but from the practical also. According to the Laws of Vibration, "like attracts like." To establish a perfect physical channel for the highest vibrations of Universal Life Energy to flow through, enabling it to become a powerful magnetic center for Universal Harmony to manifest itself in, only the finest materials could be used.

Everyone in possession of this book will soon discover that merely to possess it is to have established a connecting link between Universal Life Energy and the individual who owns the book, or the house or office where it is kept. It is advisable to carry the book with oneself whenever a business transaction or any important step is contemplated. The book will always act as an inspiring harmonizing and protecting agent because of its actual connection with the pure magnetic vibrations of Universal Life Energy.

The size, thinness and lightness of the book make it most convenient to carry in one's vest pocket or handbag. The width of the book is four inches, which number stands for the Four Fundamentals of All Being: Life, Mind, Truth and Love. Its length is seven inches, representing the Complete Round of the Seven Cycles of Humanity's Evolution.

If properly cared for the book will not only retain its magnetic power, but will become more magnetic with the passing of time.

When writing in the book, the owner must be particular to use brown or golden ink, thus to keep in harmony with the unity of its color scheme. To use ink of another color would mean to bring out the Law of Polarity, which the author has so carefully avoided.

The emblem of the "Science of Being," is represented on the cover of the book by three six-pointed stars, one within the other, and a central balanced cross.

The six-pointed star is the Star of Wisdom: the three stars, one within another, Wisdom on the Three Planes – Physical, Mental and Spiritual.

"Lightbearer Emblem"
Written by Eugene Fersen

Artwork a collaboration between Eugene Fersen and Malcolm Thurnburn

    The emblem of the "Science of Being" is a representation of three six-pointed stars, one within the other, and a central balanced cross. The six-pointed is the Star of Wisdom; the three stars, one within another, Wisdom on the Three Planes - Physical, Mental and Spiritual.

    The six rays of the outer star have the appearance of Wings, the feathers of which are Magnetic Vibrations - They stand for Life Energy.

    Two interlaced equilateral triangles, forming the Seal of Solomon (Wisdom, Equilibrium, Male and Female Principles combined as one), make the second six-pointed star. A circular halo representing Mental Vibrations surrounds it.

    The six rays, perfect triangles, also each one representing creation on three planes, stand for the six cycles of humanity's evolution, often allegorically called the six days of creation.

    The lowest ray of the Star expresses the first day-the separation of light from darkness, the discrimination through Understanding between right and wrong.

    To the right, the next ray shows the creation of water and the firmament, which means energy, becomes active under the impulse from above.

The third or lower left ray shows the creation of the dry land, with its plant life - Fundamental Principles manifested, with the first sign of life activity.

The fourth or upper right shows the appearance of the Sun, Moon, and Stars, Universal Powers becoming discernible, while the fifth day opposite shows the creation of birds and other forms of Lower animal life, symbolizing mind progressing through knowledge of Human-Laws in its enfoldment until it is able to soar above the Earth.

The top ray of the six-pointed star shows the creation (unveiling) of Man in the Image of the Creative Principle Itself. His head and shoulders are visible. His right and left hands, powers to give and receive, extend across the birds and the sun.

His feet (fundamental activities) separate the globes of Light and Darkness. The man is crowded and haloed with Rays of Light (Knowledge), and his six great wings (sustaining life Energy), spread out on all sides, forming the first six-pointed star of Magnetic Vibrations. The central six-pointed star covering the body (Inner Activities) of man, is made of flashes of lightning which emanate from the center, forming a small balanced Cross.

"May The Flame Of Love Always Light Your Path"

~ Next Generation Lightbearers ~

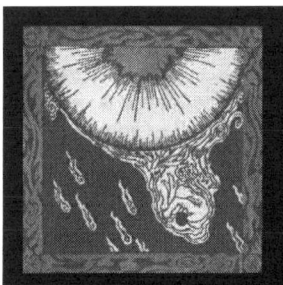

"Birth of the Absolute Spirit"

The Sun (Center) of all Life, Intelligence, Truth and Love, from which individual Mind (Man) with his followers is breaking away (separation from the Great Principle, called the Fall of Man).

Lesson 1 of the Science of Being Course.

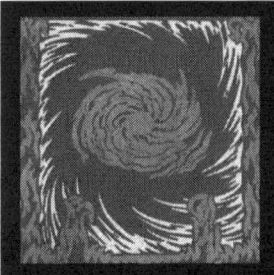

"Life Energy I"

Life Energy as the Fundamental Power of all Creation: evolving a world.

Lesson 2 of the Science of Being Course.

"The Relative Matter"

The Human brain within a skull, pictured as a scroll within a temple. The Seven Laws are represented as seven golden flames guarding the entrance to the temple. Mind involved in Matter. Material interpretation of the Eternal Reality. The teachings of the incarnate soul.

Lesson 3 of the Science of Being Course.

"Life Energy II"

The dispersing vapors (of Ignorance) disclosing the heavenly bodies (Eternal Powers).

Lesson 4 of the Science of Being Course.

"Laws, Absolute and Relative"

The soaring of the human mind as birds into higher regions; the breaking away from material concepts through the Knowledge of Eternal Laws.

Lesson 5 of the Science of Being Course.

"Mind Force"

Mind (Man) revealed as a mighty spirit inspired from above, surrounded by Light (Knowledge) emerging from the clouds of Ignorance and Superstition

Lesson 6 of the Science of Being Course.

"Spiritual Power"

Perfect beings complete spheres, dwelling in Eternal Light, ascending throughout Eternity, through Infinite Space.

Lesson 7 of the Science of Being Course.

"Assistance from the Divine Principle"

This art work shows the Absolute Spirit, God our Father who is also our loving Mother - sending down to Earth the vibrations of the Laws of Love, with the hope that Humanity will re-remember what they are innately - Supreme Heavenly Beings.

"Love & Inspiration"

This art work, a bowl with a flame being held up by two hands is known to the Lightbearers as "The Flame of Love and Inspiration."

All artwork a collaboration between Eugene Fersen and Malcolm Thurnburn

"The Mighty Spirit"

Mind-Man represented as a mighty spirit, six-winged being, floating through luminous space, the flame of Inspiration over his head, his feet resting on rays of light (Knowledge), and his hands holding the six-pointed Star of Wisdom.

Artwork a collaboration between Eugene Fersen and Malcolm Thurnburn

"The Awakening"

Man (Mind) having completed his cycle of evolution, rising on his wings of Inspiration amidst Rays of Light (Knowledge) toward the Supreme Goal, Perfection represented by a Seven-Pointed Star. The sentence below the illustration: "It was but a dream, and now you are awake," means that when liberated from the dream of Ignorance and Superstition, Man (Mind) will awake to the Realities of Eternal and Boundless Life.

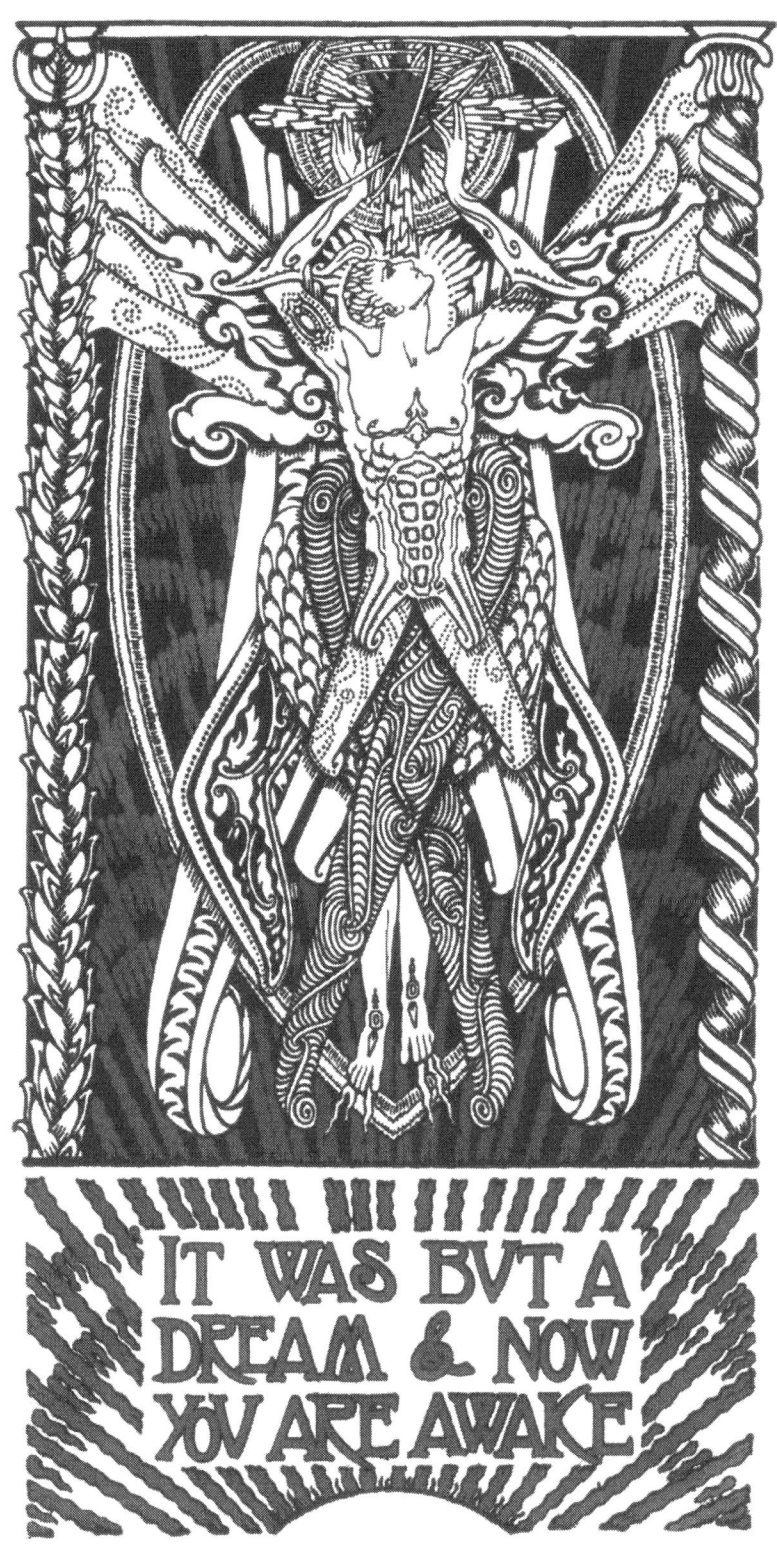

Artwork a collaboration between Eugene Fersen and Malcolm Thurnburn

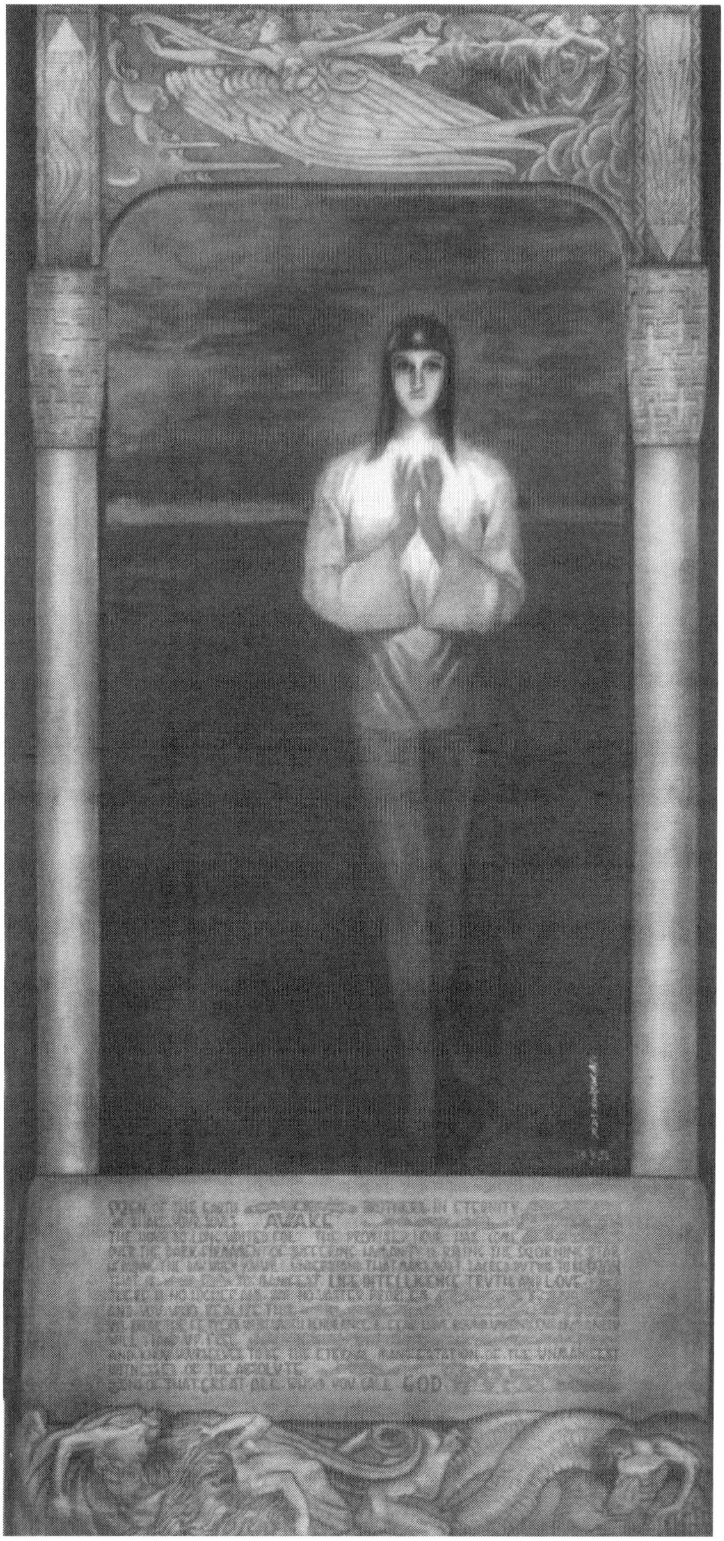
BROTHERS IN ETERNITY
AWAKE
GOD

THE MORNING STAR
"The Picture with a Soul,"

A collaborative artwork of both Malcolm Thurnburn and the Princess Marie Eristoff-Kasak

This picture is considered the masterpiece of Princess M. Eristoff, a renowned Russian artist, member of the French National Society of Fine Arts, in Paris, whose wonderfully living portraits and extraordinary mystic subjects have won high honors in the annual exhibits at the French "Salon." It was painted during the first years of the Great War, at the request of Baron Eugene Fersen, of Moscow, Russia, its present owner. It represents, in allegorical form, the transition NOW in process in the evolution of Humanity.

Profound night envelops the desolate earth. A few stars smolder dully through the blanketing clouds, and intensify the oppressive gloom below. Across the dreary waste comes a Being clad in white, his serene countenance illumined by the light he bears before him, his eyes fixed upon Infinity and Eternity. And through his eyes Infinity and Eternity look out upon the world. The helmet that encircles his brow is as if carved from the deep blue of an untarnished firmament, and holds written in its gleams Determination and Inspiration from above. His simple garment of white is lustrous with Purity of Purpose. And the light cradled in his strong hands is the Morning Star, Herald of the New Day, whose approaching glory even now stains the remote horizon with a greenish glow of promise. A golden cross flames in the heart of the Star, standing united with it as the emblem of the New Era, in which Love purifies Mind, and Gentleness refines Energy. Broad are the shoulders of this Bearer of Light – broad enough to carry the burden of the whole world – and bare are his strong limbs. No coverings guard his feet from the sharp stones that strew his path, blunt the keen fangs of heat and cold and storms; yet his steps do not falter; he moves tranquilly on, strong in the knowledge of his mission, dispelling the mists and obscurity by the radiant splendor of the Star. At the touch of his bruised foot spring forth bluebells, ringing joy to the hearts of men and his blood waters a flowery trail for those who will follow. On the stone panel beneath his feet is engraved the great message he brings to the world. "Men of the Earth, Brother in Eternity, arouse your souls! AWAKE! The hour so long waited for, the promised hour, has come. Over the dark firmament of suffering Humanity is rising the Morning Star, heralding the day when you will understand that man's most sacred duty is to be Man – that is, to manifest Life, Intelligence, Truth, and Love. There is no higher aim, no vaster problem, and those who realize this will break the fetters with which Ignorance and Fear have bound unconscious Humanity, will stand up free, and know themselves to be the Eternal Manifestation of the Unmanifest, Witnesses of the Great ALL, Sons of the Absolute, whom you call God."

This realization brings to man powers before unknown, because so great. The four giants who serve Nature, the Elements – Air, Fire, Earth, and Water – are laid prostrate at his feet, dominated by him.

The two aspects of the Star – Phosphorus, the Morning Star, the Star of Gladness, announcing to Humanity the glorious birth of a new day, and Hesperus, the Evening Star, the star of mystery and sadness, warning Humanity of the approaching darkness – unite to form henceforth a single Star. And, on the side of Hesperus, a triangle, falling amid streaks of lightening, symbolizes Humanity's involution, while on the other side, the side of Light, is seen the flame of Love lifting the same human triangle back to the realm of Eternal Harmony. A dark swastika, protected by the fiery cross, adorns the left capital of the two pillars a further symbol of the same idea of involution, and is contrasted to the luminous swastika of evolution which burns from the shadow of the same cross on the right capital.

Malcolm Thurburn, the author of this mystical frame is an English artist whose novel and original ideas have created a great sensation in America and in Europe. Both artists, Princess Eristoff and Malcolm Thurburn, have embodied their very souls in this picture, and thereby endowed it with an extraordinary appeal which mere technical perfection could never impart. The more one sees it, the more fascinating it grows, a living messenger to those who possess it, of wonderful times to come. It is a picture, which brings blessings and harmony to the homes where it abides. And above all, it is a real companion, because it is A PICTURE WITH A SOUL.

Made in the USA
Charleston, SC
15 October 2013